# SpringerBriefs in Computer Science

SpringerBriefs present concise summaries of cutting-edge research and practical applications across a wide spectrum of fields. Featuring compact volumes of 50 to 125 pages, the series covers a range of content from professional to academic.

Typical topics might include:

- A timely report of state-of-the art analytical techniques
- A bridge between new research results, as published in journal articles, and a contextual literature review
- A snapshot of a hot or emerging topic
- An in-depth case study or clinical example
- A presentation of core concepts that students must understand in order to make independent contributions.

Briefs allow authors to present their ideas and readers to absorb them with minimal time investment. Briefs will be published as part of Springer's eBook collection, with millions of users worldwide. In addition, Briefs will be available for individual print and electronic purchase. Briefs are characterized by fast, global electronic dissemination, standard publishing contracts, easy-to-use manuscript preparation and formatting guidelines, and expedited production schedules. We aim for publication 8–12 weeks after acceptance. Both solicited and unsolicited manuscripts are considered for publication in this series.

**Indexing: This series is indexed in Scopus, Ei-Compendex, and zbMATH **

Richard Comploi-Taupe · Andreas Falkner

# Product Configuration

## An Introduction for Practitioners

**SIEMENS**

 Springer

Richard Comploi-Taupe
Siemens AG Österreich
Vienna, Austria

Andreas Falkner
Vienna, Austria

ISSN 2191-5768 ISSN 2191-5776 (electronic)
SpringerBriefs in Computer Science
ISBN 978-3-032-17162-7 ISBN 978-3-032-17163-4 (eBook)
https://doi.org/10.1007/978-3-032-17163-4

This work was supported by Siemens Aktiengesellschaft Österreich.

© Siemens Aktiengesellschaft Österreich 2026. This book is an open access publication.

**Open Access** This book is licensed under the terms of the Creative Commons Attribution-NonCommercial-NoDerivatives 4.0 International License (http://creativecommons.org/licenses/by-nc-nd/4.0/), which permits any noncommercial use, sharing, distribution and reproduction in any medium or format, as long as you give appropriate credit to the original author(s) and the source, provide a link to the Creative Commons license and indicate if you modified the licensed material. You do not have permission under this license to share adapted material derived from this book or parts of it.

The images or other third party material in this book are included in the book's Creative Commons license, unless indicated otherwise in a credit line to the material. If material is not included in the book's Creative Commons license and your intended use is not permitted by statutory regulation or exceeds the permitted use, you will need to obtain permission directly from the copyright holder.

This work is subject to copyright. All commercial rights are reserved by the author(s), whether the whole or part of the material is concerned, specifically the rights of translation, reprinting, reuse of illustrations, recitation, broadcasting, reproduction on microfilms or in any other physical way, and transmission or information storage and retrieval, electronic adaptation, computer software, or by similar or dissimilar methodology now known or hereafter developed. Regarding these commercial rights a non-exclusive license has been granted to the publisher.

The use of general descriptive names, registered names, trademarks, service marks, etc. in this publication does not imply, even in the absence of a specific statement, that such names are exempt from the relevant protective laws and regulations and therefore free for general use.

The publisher, the authors and the editors are safe to assume that the advice and information in this book are believed to be true and accurate at the date of publication. Neither the publisher nor the authors or the editors give a warranty, expressed or implied, with respect to the material contained herein or for any errors or omissions that may have been made. The publisher remains neutral with regard to jurisdictional claims in published maps and institutional affiliations.

This Springer imprint is published by the registered company Springer Nature Switzerland AG
The registered company address is: Gewerbestrasse 11, 6330 Cham, Switzerland

If disposing of this product, please recycle the paper.

# Preface

This book offers an introduction to the field of product configuration. It is designed for industry practitioners interested in the practical aspects of product configuration, as well as students seeking to learn about or conduct research in this domain.

It aims to equip readers with the ability to:

- Understand the benefits of diverse forms of individualization of products, including Product Configuration, Mass Customization, and Product Line Engineering, and
- Effectively model configuration problems using appropriate tools such as UML class diagrams, feature models, and logic programming.

The authors bring extensive experience to this book, having worked for many years—Andreas for over three decades—at Siemens' research department. Their work has encompassed developing product configurators for various Siemens business units, supporting product managers in tool selection, conducting research on configuration technologies, and teaching configuration-related courses for students at the University of Klagenfurt and at the Graz University of Technology in Austria.

Through this book, we aim to share our accumulated experience and knowledge. Consequently, it presents product configuration from a practical perspective, with a strong emphasis on knowledge-based approaches.

## How to Read this Book

The initial chapters of this book provide an overview of the topic. After a general introduction which also sets the terminology and outlines the benefits (Chap. 1), we cover the scope of product configuration (Chap. 2) and the business context, including architectures and interfaces to other systems (Chap. 3). There is a separate chapter on modeling (Chap. 4) and one providing an overview of configuration technologies (Chap. 5). Towards the end of the book, chapters address the main challenges in practice: quality (Chap. 6) and performance tuning (Chap. 7). Finally, two chapters provide insights into important current research directions: Chap. 8 describes how Generative AI approaches such as large language models (LLMs), chatbots, foundation models, and similar technologies could be utilized as user interfaces for configurators in the future or to support configuration processes in other ways; and Chap. 9 addresses the incorporation of sustainability and lifecycle information in product configurators.

We tried to keep each chapter self-contained so that readers who already know a little about product configuration can start with any chapter. However, we suggest reading Chap. 4 (modeling) before Chaps. 5–9. For beginners, we recommend following the chapters from start to end and choosing from the more specialized chapters (beginning with Chap. 6) only those of interest to them.

All chapters contain examples and exercises to support the reader's learning journey. The purpose of these exercises is in most cases to deepen the reader's understanding of the chapter, for example, by applying the covered topics in practice. In some cases, exercises assist the reader in building additional knowledge through small research tasks, aided by literature references.

## What this Book is not About

This is a short book, and we had to omit several interesting topics. Here, we provide a selection of topics relevant to product configuration that are not covered by this book, along with references to relevant literature. For an even wider range of configuration-related topics along with references to literature, we refer the reader to a survey by Zhang [36].

**Object-oriented configuration** addresses object-oriented aspects that significantly shape many real-world configuration problems, and discusses how to model and solve them [1, 2, 8, 10, 30, 33, 35].

**System configuration** concerns the configuration of large systems that consist of several subsystems [4, 28, 32].

**Production configuration** involves configuring not only products but also the production facilities and processes used to produce them [5–7, 34].

**Optimization** in solving technology focuses on finding optimal solutions (configurations) [18, 24–26].

**Diagnosis** is a technique relevant for several purposes in product configuration, including harmonizing inconsistent user requirements and debugging configuration models [12–15, 17, 22, 27, 29].

**Interactive configuration** pertains to efficiently guiding a user through a configuration process [9, 16, 19, 20].

## Additional Resources

Much of the content of this book is original work by the authors, based upon extensive sources in scientific literature and commercial vendor information, whether in written form or as presented at conferences and workshops. We recommend the following resources for further information.

Books:

- Knowledge-based Configuration: From Research to Business Cases [13]
- Product Customization [21]
- The chapter on *Configuration* in the Handbook of Constraint Programming [23]
- Feature Models: AI-Driven Design, Analysis and Applications [11]

Academic conferences and workshops:

- International Workshop on Configuration:[1] *the* regular academic meeting of the configuration community
- Changeable, Agile, Reconfigurable and Virtual Production Conference (CARV), World Mass Customization and Personalization Conference (MCPC): conferences on agile production, mass customization, and customer co-creation
- ACM International Systems and Software Product Line Conference (SPLC): a conference on product line engineering
- International Working Conference on Variability Modeling of Software-Intensive Systems (VaMoS): a conference on variability modeling

Journals:

- Artificial Intelligence for Engineering Design, Analysis and Manufacturing (AI EDAM):[2] has published several special issues on Configuration
- IEEE Intelligent Systems:[3] has published several articles on Configuration, e.g., the special edition [31] is a collection which provides a good overview of the whole domain
- International Journal of Mass Customisation (IJMC):[4] a journal dedicated to the field of Mass Customization and related topics

Another valuable resource is Cyledge's Configurator Database[5] [3], a collection of web-based sales configurators.

---

[1] https://confws.github.io/history/.

[2] https://www.cambridge.org/core/journals/ai-edam.

[3] https://www.computer.org/csdl/magazine/ex.

[4] https://www.inderscience.com/jhome.php?jcode=ijmassc.

[5] https://www.configurator-database.com/.

## Acknowledgements

Both authors have been able to write a significant portion of this book within their working time at Siemens. Furthermore, Siemens has generously sponsored the book's open-access publication to support its free availability to readers worldwide. All of this would not have been possible without the support of Herwig Schreiner, who heads our research group. Thank you very much!

We are grateful to our contributing writers: Chap. 8 is based on a workshop paper by Philipp Kogler, Wei Chen, Andreas Falkner, Alois Haselböck, and Stefan Wallner, who kindly permitted us to use their work and contributed to its revision for inclusion in this book. Chapter 9 is based on a workshop paper by Gottfried Schenner, Giray Havur, Sophie Rogenhofer, Stefan Wallner, Erwin Filtz, and Tassilo Pellegrini, who kindly permitted us to use their work and contributed to its revision for inclusion in this book. Ruben Liedy provided input on the topic of user experience in Chap 6.

Work on Chap. 9 has been partially funded by the Austrian Research Promotion Agency (FFG) under the project grants FO999915294 (ECO-TCO) and FO999917177 (PACE-DPP).

We thank the following readers for their valuable feedback on earlier drafts of this book at various stages of the writing process: Prof. Gerhard Friedrich from the University of Klagenfurt; Prof. Alexander Felfernig from Graz University of Technology; our colleagues Jonas Pettersson, Philipp Kogler, Wei Chen, Stefan Wallner, and Gottfried Schenner; and the participants of the university courses *Knowledge-based Product Configuration* (University of Klagenfurt, winter semester 2024/25) and *Configuration Systems* (Graz University of Technology, winter semester 2024/25).

The names of the authors of this book are ordered alphabetically.

<table>
<tr><td>Vienna, Austria</td><td align="right">Richard Comploi-Taupe</td></tr>
<tr><td>October 2025</td><td align="right">Andreas Falkner</td></tr>
</table>

## References

1. Bak, K., Diskin, Z., Antkiewicz, M., Czarnecki, K., Wasowski, A.: Clafer: unifying class and feature modeling. Softw. Syst. Model. **15**(3), 811–845 (2016). https://doi.org/10.1007/S10270-014-0441-1

2. Balážová, L., Comploi-Taupe, R., Hahn, S., Rühling, N., Schenner, G.: Smart expansion techniques for ASP-based interactive configuration. Theory Pract. Log. Program. (2025). https://doi.org/10.1017/S147106842510029X

3. cyLEDGE Media: Configurator database (2022). https://www.configurator-database.com/

4. Dhungana, D., Falkner, A.A., Haselböck, A.: Generation of conjoint domain models for system-of-systems. In: J. Järvi, C. Kästner (eds.) Generative Programming: Concepts and Experiences, GPCE'13, Indianapolis, IN, USA—October 27–28, 2013, pp. 159–168. ACM (2013). https://doi.org/10.1145/2517208.2517224

5. Dhungana, D., Falkner, A.A., Haselböck, A., Taupe, R.: Enabling integrated product and factory configuration in smart production ecosystems. In: 43rd Euromicro Conference on Software Engineering and Advanced Applications, SEAA 2017, Vienna, Austria, 30 Aug–1 Sept 2017, pp. 266–273. IEEE Computer Society (2017). https://doi.org/10.1109/SEAA.2017.26

6. Dhungana, D., Haselböck, A., Taupe, R.: A marketplace for smart production ecosystems. In: Hankammer, S., Nielsen, K., Piller, F.T., Schuh, G., Wang, N. (eds.) Customization 4.0, pp. 103–123. Springer, Cham (2018)

7. Dhungana, D., Haselböck, A., Wallner, S.: Generation of multi-factory production plans: enabling collaborative lot-size-one production. In: 46th Euromicro Conference on Software Engineering and Advanced Applications, SEAA 2020, Portoroz, Slovenia, 26–28 Aug 2020, pp. 529–536. IEEE, USA (2020). https://doi.org/10.1109/SEAA51224.2020.00088

8. Falkner, A., Feinerer, I., Salzer, G., Schenner, G.: Computing product configurations via UML and integer linear programming. Int. J. Mass Cust. 3(4), 351–367 (2010)

9. Falkner, A.A., Haselböck, A., Krames, G., Schenner, G., Schreiner, H., Taupe, R.: Solver requirements for interactive configuration. J. Univers. Comput. Sci. 26(3), 343–373 (2020). http://www.jucs.org/jucs_26_3/solver_requirements_for_interactive

10. Falkner, A.A., Ryabokon, A., Schenner, G., Shchekotykhin, K.M.: OOASP: connecting object oriented and logic programming. In: Calimeri, F., Ianni, G., Truszczynski M. (eds.) Logic Programming and Nonmonotonic Reasoning—13th International Conference, LPNMR 2015, Lexington, KY, USA, 27–30 Sept 2015. In: Proceedings, Lecture Notes in Computer Science, vol. 9345, pp. 332–345. Springer, Berlin (2015). https://doi.org/10.1007/978-3-319-23264-5_28

11. Felfernig, A., Falkner, A., Benavides, D.: Feature models: AI-driven design, analysis and applications. In: Springer Briefs in Computer Science. Springer, Cham (2024). https://doi.org/10.1007/978-3-031-61874-1

12. Felfernig, A., Friedrich, G., Jannach, D., Stumptner, M.: Consistency-based diagnosis of configuration knowledge bases. Artif. Intell. 152(2), 213–234 (2004)

13. Felfernig, A., Hotz, L., Bagley, C., Tiihonen, J. (eds.): Knowledge-Based Configuration: From Research to Business Cases, 1st edn. Morgan Kaufmann Publishers Inc., San Francisco, CA (2014). ISBN: 2415817X

14. Felfernig, A., Reiterer, S., Reinfrank, F., Ninaus, G., Jeran, M.: Conflict detection and diagnosis in configuration. In: Felfernig et al. [13], Chap. 7, pp. 73–87

15. Felfernig, A., Walter, R., Galindo, J.A., Benavides, D., Erdeniz, S.P., Atas, M., Reiterer, S.: Anytime diagnosis for reconfiguration. J. Intell. Inf. Syst. 51(1), 161–182 (2018). https://doi.org/10.1007/S10844-017-0492-1

16. Freuder, E.C., O'Sullivan, B.: Generating tradeoffs for interactive constraint-based configuration. In: Walsh, T. (ed.) Principles and Practice of Constraint Programming—CP 2001, 7th International Conference, CP 2001, Paphos, Cyprus, 26 Nov–1 Dec 2001, Proceedings, Lecture Notes in Computer Science, vol. 2239, pp. 590–594. Springer, Berlin (2001). https://doi.org/10.1007/3-540-45578-7_45

17. Friedrich, G., Jannach, D., Stumptner, M., Zanker, M.: Knowledge engineering for configuration systems. In: Felfernig et al. [13], Chap. 11, pp. 139–155

18. Garces, L., Pitiot, P., Monge, L.G., Vareilles, É.: Towards a benchmark for configuration and planning optimization problems. In: Tiihonen, J., Falkner, A.A., Axling T. (eds.) Proceedings of the 17th International Configuration Workshop, Vienna, Austria, 10–11 Sept 2015, CEUR Workshop Proceedings, vol. 1453, pp. 61–65. CEUR-WS.org (2015). https://ceur-ws.org/Vol-1453/10_MongePitiotAldanondoVareilles_TowardsABenchmarkForConfiguration_Confws-15_p61.pdf

19. Haag, A., Riemann, S.: Product configuration as decision support: the declarative paradigm in practice. Artif. Intell. Eng. Des. Anal. Manuf. 25(2), 131–142 (2011). https://doi.org/10.1017/S0890060410000582

20. Hertum, P.V., Dasseville, I., Janssens, G., Denecker, M.: The KB paradigm and its application to interactive configuration. Theory Pract. Log. Program. 17(1), 91–117 (2017). https://doi.org/10.1017/S1471068416000156

21. Hvam, L., Mortensen, N.H., Riis, J.: Product Customization. Springer, Berlin (2008)
22. Junker, U.: QUICKXPLAIN: preferred explanations and relaxations for over-constrained problems. In: McGuinness, D.L., Ferguson, G. (eds.) Proceedings of the Nineteenth National Conference on Artificial Intelligence, Sixteenth Conference on Innovative Applications of Artificial Intelligence, 25–29 July 2004, San Jose, California, USA, pp. 167–172. AAAI Press/The MIT Press (2004). http://www.aaai.org/Library/AAAI/2004/aaai04-027.php
23. Junker, U.: Configuration. In: Rossi, F., van Beek, P., Walsh T. (eds.) Handbook of Constraint Programming, pp. 837–873. Elsevier Science (2006)
24. Legriel, J., Guernic, C.L., Cotton, S., Maler, O.: Approximating the pareto front of multi-criteria optimization problems. In: Esparza, J., Majumdar, R. (eds.) Tools and Algorithms for the Construction and Analysis of Systems, 16th International Conference, TACAS 2010, Held as Part of the Joint European Conferences on Theory and Practice of Software, ETAPS 2010, Paphos, Cyprus, 20–28 Mar 2010. Proceedings, Lecture Notes in Computer Science, vol. 6015, pp. 69–83. Springer, Berlin (2010). https://doi.org/10.1007/978-3-642-12002-2_6
25. Oh, J., Batory, D., Heradio, R.: Finding near-optimal configurations in colossal spaces with statistical guarantees. ACM Trans. Softw. Eng. Methodol. **33**(1), 1–36 (2023)
26. Pitiot, P., Aldanondo, M., Vareilles, E., Gaborit, P., Djefel, M., Carbonnel, S.: Concurrent product configuration and process planning, towards an approach combining interactivity and optimality. Int. J. Prod. Res. **51**(2), 524–541 (2013). DOI 10.1080/00207543. 2011.653449
27. Reiter, R.: A theory of diagnosis from first principles. Artif. Intell. **32**(1), 57–95 (1987). https://doi.org/10.1016/0004-3702(87)90062-2
28. Rigger, E., Stankovic, T., Fleisch, R.: Facilitating configuration model formalization based on systems engineering. In: Aldanondo, M., Falkner, A.A., Felfernig, A., Stettinger M. (eds.) Proceedings of the 23rd International Configuration Workshop (CWS/ConfWS 2021), Vienna, Austria, 16–17 Sept 2021, CEUR Workshop Proceedings, vol. 2945, pp. 1–8. CEUR-WS.org (2021). URL https://ceur-ws.org/Vol-2945/11-ER-ConfWS21_paper_14.pdf
29. Rodler, P.: A formal proof and simple explanation of the quickxplain algorithm. Artif. Intell. Rev. **55**(8), 6185–6206 (2022). https://doi.org/10.1007/S10462-022-10149-W
30. Schenner, G., Taupe, R.: Encoding object-oriented models in MiniZinc. In: 15th International Workshop on Constraint Modelling and Reformulation (ModRef'16) (2016). http://cp2016. a4cp.org/program/workshops/ws-modref-papers/Taupe.pdf
31. Sinz, C., Haag, A., Narodytska, N., Walsh, T., Gelle, E., Sabin, M., Junker, U., O'Sullivan, B., Rabiser, R., Dhungana, D., Grunbacher, P., Lehner, K., Federspiel, C., Naus, D.: Configuration. IEEE Intell. Syst. **22**(1), 78–90 (2007). https://doi.org/10.1109/MIS.2007.6
32. Sylla, A., Guillon, D., Ayachi, R., Vareilles, É., Aldanondo, M., Coudert, T., Geneste, L.: How to deal with engineering-to-order product/system configuration? In: Felfernig, A., Tiihonen, J., Hotz, L., Stettinger M. (eds.) Proceedings of the 20th Configuration Workshop, Graz, Austria, 27–28 Sept 2018, CEUR Workshop Proceedings, vol. 2220, pp. 103–108. CEUR-WS.org (2018). https://ceur-ws.org/Vol-2220/17_CONFWS18_paper_22.pdf
33. Tack, G., Comploi-Taupe, R., Falkner, A., Schenner, G.: MiniZinc with objects. Constraints (2025). https://doi.org/10.1007/s10601-025-09380-3
34. Taupe, R., Falkner, A.: Production reconfiguration with ASP. In: Proceedings of the 22nd International Configuration Workshop, pp. 39–46. Università degli Studi di Padova (2020). https://www.eventhelpr.com/files/events/RqdLM1Pt/attachments/procee dings-cws-2020_JEqWr6vY.pdf
35. Taupe, R., Falkner, A., Schenner, G.: Deriving tighter component cardinality bounds for product configuration. In: 18th International Configuration Workshop, pp. 47–54 (2016). http://cp2016.a4cp.org/program/workshops/CWS-2016-Proceedings.pdf
36. Zhang, L.: Product configuration: a reviewof the state-of-the-art and future research. Int. J. Prod. Res. **52**, 6381–6398 (2014). https://doi.org/10.1080/00207543.2014.942012

# Contents

# Acronyms

ASP    Answer Set Programming
ATO    Assemble-to-Order
BOM    Bill of Materials
BOP    Bill of Processes
BTS    Build-To-Stock
CAD    Computer-Aided Design
CLM    Configuration Lifecycle Management
CP    Constraint Programming
CPQ    Configure, Price, Quote
CRM    Customer Relationship Management
CSP    Constraint Satisfaction Problem
CTO    Configure-To-Order
DPP    Digital Product Passport
DSL    Domain-Specific Language
EPD    Environmental Product Declaration
ERP    Enterprise Resource Planning
ESPR    Ecodesign for Sustainable Products Regulation
ETO    Engineer-To-Order
FM    Feature Modeling
FOL    First-Order Logic
GWP    Global Warming Potential
ISO    International Standardization Organization
KRR    Knowledge Representation and Reasoning
LCA    Life Cycle Assessment
LLM    Large Language Model
MC    Mass Customization
MES    Manufacturing Execution System
NLP    Natural Language Processing
PC    Product Configuration
PDM    Product Data Management
PEF    Product Environmental Footprint

PLE      Product Line Engineering
PLM      Product Lifecycle Management
PTO      Pick-To-Order
SCM      Supply Chain Management
VM       Variability Management

# Chapter 1
# Introduction

**Abstract** Product configuration is the activity of customizing a product to meet the individual needs of a particular customer. The goal is to offer such a product at a similar price as in mass production and to transparently give the customer all relevant information, e.g., about environmental impact. This requires appropriate tools, i.e. configurators, for specifying the product variety and recommending individual solutions. This chapter introduces the most important concepts and terms around product configuration to lay a solid basis for the book. The historical development of the subject matter is outlined briefly, various degrees of individualization are discussed, important stakeholders are listed, and the importance and benefits of mass customization and product configuration for modern manufacturing are motivated. In the end of the chapter, we introduce the configurable folding bike product that will serve as running example throughout the book.

How can one best start an introductory book about product configuration? There are so many aspects in this topic, such as definition of terms, scope, context, benefits, technologies. Understanding each of them depends on understanding all the others. And each reader comes with their own interests and previous knowledge. In fact, reading the book can be seen as the configuration of an individual reading experience: select the chapters where to start and continue, skip or repeat certain parts, follow references, work on exercises. And writing the book can be seen as modeling the potential experiences for different readers: specify the content, group it in digestible sections, supply supporting diagrams and figures, design exercises (because humans will truly understand only if they try themselves).[1]

---

[1] Already the Confucian philosophers in ancient China knew: Tell me and I will forget, show me and I may remember, let me do and I will understand. (https://quoteinvestigator.com/2019/02/27/tell/).

© Siemens Aktiengesellschaft Österreich 2026

R. Comploi-Taupe and A. Falkner, *Product Configuration*,
SpringerBriefs in Computer Science,
https://doi.org/10.1007/978-3-032-17163-4_1

## 1.1  Terms and Definitions

There are several terms and definitions which mean more or less the same, but emphasize different aspects of product configuration:

- Product Configuration (PC): is the activity of customizing a product to the needs of a particular customer (many definitions include the aspects that configured products consist of a set of predefined components and that they need to satisfy some predefined constraints [25, 28])
- System or Solution Configuration: extends the product configuration concepts to huge products in a broad sense, i.e., those which comprise several subsystems or many components, or are a collection of related smaller products
- CPQ System: means Configure—Price—Quote, making clear that not only configuration (in a narrow sense) is covered by the tool, but also calculation of prices and generation of documents
- Sales Configurator: is a configuration tool responsible for creating a binding offer, used by a sales person (including back office) or directly by an end-customer
- Guided Selling: emphasizes the method of guiding a user to find efficiently what they are looking for, starting with questions oriented towards the real needs of the customer instead of technical parameters
- Mass Customization (MC—a term introduced 1987 by Davis [4], later driven by Pine [22] and Piller [21]): puts the efficient production of customized products in focus (combination of mass production and customization)
- Product Line Engineering (PLE): refers to the specification and maintenance of a product family, i.e., feasible variants of a configurable product
- Variability Management (VM): highlights that the variants of a product need to be designed and controlled continuously [3, 11, 18, 23, 24].

Other terms relate to product configuration or describe technologies which can be exploited for it:

- Lot-size-one Production: is a main goal of the Industry 4.0 initiative [2] and can be enabled by mass customization
- Recommender System: is a technology to help configurator users to efficiently satisfy their requirements by recommending products or variants that most probably align with the customer's needs
- Mathematical Optimization: is a set of technologies to find optimal solutions to a variety of problems
- Model-Driven Engineering: offers concepts and tools to specify assets of any kind, including configurable products
- Modularization & Standardization: are means to make products easier to customize
- Generative Design: leaves the consumer in control of the selection of a design from a large set of possibilities, while satisfying production and engineering constraints [19].

Although sometimes used as a synonym for product configuration, the term "configuration management" means a different thing: the versioning of software components, which could be parts of the product model (the product line specification). This is especially important if the product is large or a system and thus consists of different modules or subsystems which are maintained by different groups of developers. The term "configuration lifecycle management" (CLM) is used, mainly by one vendor (Configit),[2] to express the importance of configuration for the whole product lifecycle [1] (see Sect. 3.2).

## 1.2  History of Product Configuration and Mass Customization

After craftspeople had manufactured products tailor-made to the individual needs of their customers for centuries, the first and second industrial revolutions (based on steam engines and electricity, respectively) supported mass production starting in the mid of the 19th century. While the product variability was reduced, the number of units could be increased tremendously to serve the increase in population size. This culminated in the citation of Henry Ford in the 1920s: "Any customer can have a car painted any color that he wants so long as it is black" [7], which at first thought seems arrogance and complete ignorance of customer wishes. But it was necessary to produce the cars efficiently with low cost. And—even more important—the black color dried faster than other colors. So only with a black color could Henry Ford ensure the necessary speed of the conveyor belts. He had nearly gone bankrupt with another company which offered more variability but which just didn't pay off at that time.

Nowadays, everyone can order cars in any color they like and also with many different features. This was made possible through the third and fourth industrial revolutions (computers and the internet, respectively) which allowed for more flexibility in the offering and production around the end of the 20th century. Already in 1970, Alvin Toffler, an American futurist, suggested providing customized products and services to meet customer's special requirements with the cost and speed of standard mass production [27]. And by 1999, the computer company Dell sold 50% of their computers online, after having introduced an online configurator for computers in 1995 [5, 17].

As Fig. 1.1 indicates, such a move from mass production (of a set of different products) to mass customization (based on a common product family) requires modularization: By finding commonalities and reusing components, the variety gets structured. This typically reduces efforts and cost and may lead to new combinations which increase offering (i.e., viable variants) and business opportunities. Thus we achieve a high number of produced units at comparably low cost and with a sufficiently high variability to satisfy most customer requirements.

---

[2] https://configit.com/solutions/clm/.

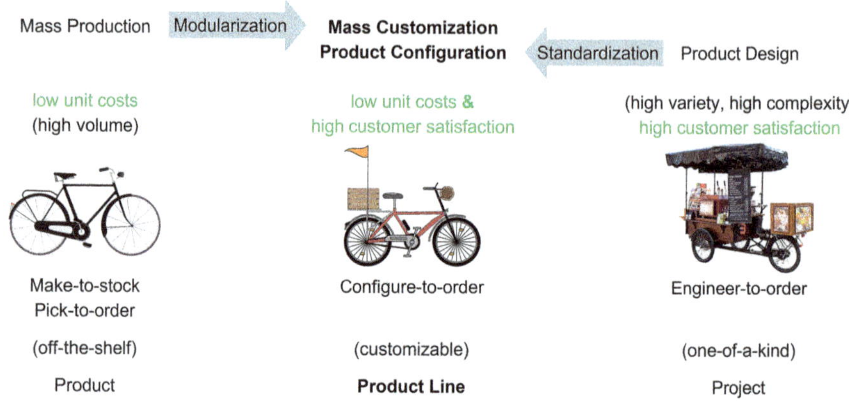



**Fig. 1.1** Product configuration for affordable individuality (*Image sources* turguthatipa/nablagrange/garten-gg)

With the power of computer systems, we can do this not only for smaller products such as computers or cars, but even for huge systems such as railroad interlocking systems, power plants, or energy distribution systems. Such products or systems are typically engineered in a one-of-a-kind approach and are more like projects than products. Standardization can help to move from product design to product configuration: Defining a standard structure (i.e., design) for a product family beforehand and removing special (i.e., non-standard) solutions from the offering reduces variability and therefore also cost. It needs to be evaluated whether making more business with the customizable product family (due to faster lead times and lower prices) pays off the potential loss of (hopefully only few) customers due to the reduced offering. Special, i.e., tailor-made and perhaps more complex solutions can still be offered outside of the standard production line, of course at a higher price.

## 1.3  Degrees of Customization and Individualization

The range of products from mass production to product design can be seen as a continuum. Figure 1.2 shows the effects on unit cost, one of the main challenges of individualization. For standard products with no or only few variants and typically lots of produced units, the unit costs are low as enabled by mass production. But for one-of-a-kind engineering or products which are produced only once, the unit costs are quite high—due to the variety that needs to be covered. The goal of mass customization is to provide highly customized products and services with the cost and speed of standard mass production. That means that mass customization is mass production plus customization. In practice, this works for many rather simple products, B2C (business-to-customer) and B2B (business-to-business). If we added

**Fig. 1.2** Mass Customization offers high variety at low unit cost (*Source* Own work)

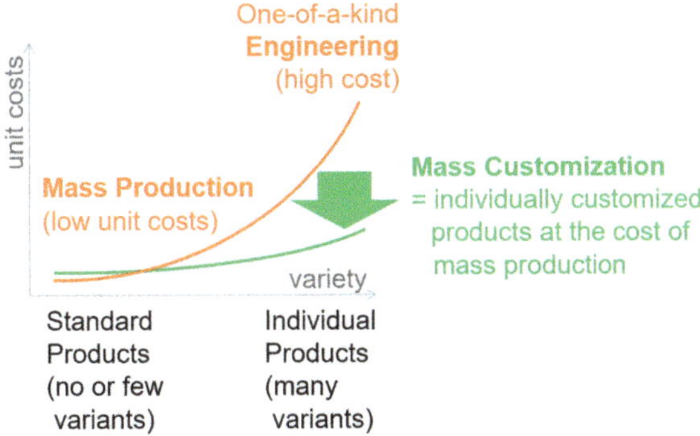



complexity of the product as a third dimension, we would see that it gets more and more difficult to bring down costs the more complex the products are.

Mass production serves market push, i.e., first make then sell. This is called build-to-stock (BTS) or make-to-stock: the product is built before the final buyer has been identified.

Customization serves the market pull approach, i.e., just produce something when it was already ordered. This is also called build-to-order (BTO), meaning the product is scheduled and built only in response to a confirmed order. An example is just-in-time production for cars: When we bought a car in the late 20th century, we went to the seller and just picked a car that was already there. Nowadays we order our car via the internet or go to the seller, but customize it and the production only starts when the order has been released.[3]

Mass customization tries to benefit from the advantages of both [13]. The individualization causes higher customer satisfaction: the customers get what they really look for. The sellers don't have any stock expenses due to just-in-time production. They also produce less waste: they don't have products on stock which they will never sell. There is the opportunity to make more business with selling add-ons by reacting to customer needs right at the point of sale. To achieve this, production processes must be optimized and tailored to the requirements of flexible products. An example for a guide to manage this challenge is the product-process matrix proposed by Hayes and Wheelwright [12].

Figure 1.3 shows the continuum of these production approaches with different degrees of customization and individualization, depending on variety[4] (of the product family) and volume (i.e., the number of produced units of a product variant):

- Pick-to-Order (PTO): A bundle of components or parts with no dependencies is selected for production. This is near to Build-to-Stock (BTS) because the compo-

---

[3] To achieve faster delivery, manufacturers may decide to produce some parts or even whole base variants (those which are often ordered) in advance and just adapt them during order fulfillment, e.g., by activating a corresponding software package which is already there—see the literature on "customer order decoupling point", e.g., [3], for more details.

[4] The software product line community often uses the term *variability* instead [8].

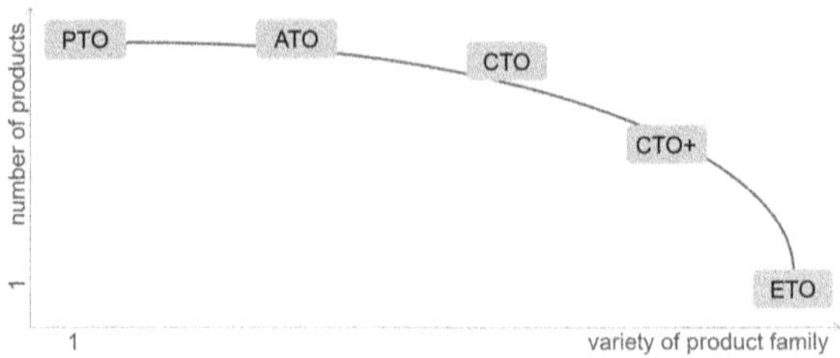



**Fig. 1.3** The continuum of build-to-order (*Source* Own work)

nents are typically prefabricated. An example is a shopping cart of a take-away restaurant where one can select the dishes for a dinner with friends.

- Assemble-to-Order (ATO): Standard components are assembled into a final product based on customer requirements. It can be seen as a mixture of BTS and BTO, as the components are made to stock, but the whole product is built to order because it is assembled only after the order is confirmed. An example is assembly of personal computers, where customers can choose from various types of components and combine them individually.
- Configure-to-Order (CTO): Components have dependencies between them, and their properties can be configured during the order process. Configurable parameters of components and a configurable structure are used to create a customized product. An example is customized software development, where customers can set various feature values and select different configurations.
- Open Configuration or CTO+: A hybrid approach between CTO and ETO, allowing users to define some details on the fly or to make small extensions to the product model during configuration. An example are industries such as door or window manufacturing, where customers can specify precise measurements in sub-millimetre sizes instead of just predefined centimetre metrics.
- Engineer-to-Order (ETO): Some components are not yet specified or known, so they need to be designed after the order is confirmed. This typically requires complex calculations and design efforts to ensure the product meets customer requirements. Examples are using a CAD-system to design a new, specific part (which is not yet in the product model) for a customized mechanical system, or newly integrating a part or component from a supplier (which does not completely comply with the existing interfaces).

A big challenge in practice is the potential explosion of the number of product variants, i.e., the size of the product family. Each alternative multiplies the numbers, e.g., a T-shirt which comes in 5 sizes, 10 colors, and 3 arm lengths (without any restrictions) spans a product family of $5 \times 10 \times 3 = 150$ variants. Proper variability management is necessary to control the resulting maintenance efforts. In Chap. 5 we take a closer look at the issue of combinatorial explosion (cf. Fig. 5.3) to give a sense of scale.

## 1.4 Stakeholders and Their Responsibilities

Proper variability management is especially important due to the involvement of many different parties and stakeholders in product configuration: product management, domain experts, knowledge engineers, tool providers, IT, sales, B2B and B2C customers, etc. Figure 1.4 gives an overview of the main roles and their responsibilities in configuration processes.

- Product manager: has the domain-specific know-how and supplies the single source of truth of all product knowledge. This is the specification of the product family and can be seen as a domain-specific problem where the product is the domain.
- Configurator user: searches an optimal solution for an individual problem instance, i.e., a set of requirements to select the best-matching product variant. Different user groups such as sales personal, business partners, or end customers need tailored support for good understanding.
- Knowledge engineer: supports the product manager to encode the domain-specific knowledge into a formal declarative representation with a clear meaning. In a similar way, the necessary input data need to be extracted from the problem instance and formalized to fit to the domain-specific model.
- Tool developer: supplies a powerful generic solver for reasoning, i.e., finding solutions to the domain-specific model, which can be tuned to the domain by the knowledge engineer. For each problem instance, the solver returns specific results, which must be translated to the user language and thus be interpreted as appropriate product variants.

In a wider context (see Chap. 3), more stakeholders are involved, e.g. from business processes such as sales, engineering, manufacturing, or delivery. They can benefit from the efforts invested into good product configuration processes.

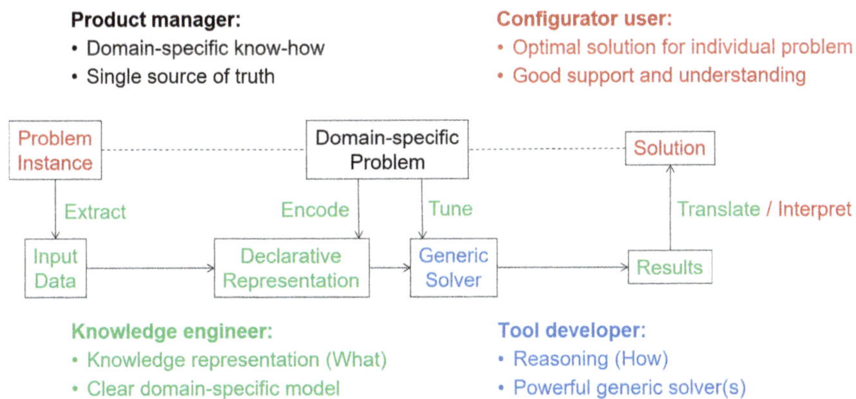


**Fig. 1.4** Stakeholders and their responsibilities in the configuration process (*Source* Own work)

## 1.5   Benefits of Product Configuration

When we want to talk about benefits, we need to first define: compared to what? For product configuration, this could be the two extreme points mentioned in Sect. 1.3: mass production and engineer-to-order. The clear advantage of product configuration over mass production is that it can fulfill individual customer requirements and it avoids unnecessary production.[5] Much more interesting is how product configuration performs better on individual production than other approaches. Therefore we will discuss in detail the benefits of CTO versus ETO.

### *Configuring Versus Engineering*

ETO processes are project-like and therefore follow a one-of-a-kind approach. This leads to some challenges, e.g., each customer requirement needs to be verified by all the involved departments. Imagine a crane seller is faced with a customer requirement to produce a crane with a boom of a certain length, e.g. 30 m. If this request is not in the standard catalogue, the salesperson needs to go to engineering to check if that length is supported by the material and structure of the crane. They might calculate that the requested length is not possible, but 28 would be allowed. So the salesperson needs to check back with the client if they can accept this suggestion. And even if so, perhaps later during delivery they'll find out that they don't have a vehicle to transport a crane of that length to the customer. Summing up, there will be feedback loops and clarifications all over the product lifecycle (cf. Fig. 1.5).

In contrast, CTO processes build on a standardized product model that has been well thought-out, tested, and documented. CTO processes are therefore more defined, clear, and smooth, compared to ETO. Here is a collection of CTO's benefits:

- Increased quality of offers and orders: A single source of truth where all product knowledge is managed and the rules and constraints which a solving engine observes guarantee correct results, i.e. feasible and even optimal products (assuming that the knowledge base is complete and consistent).
- Reduced lead time/time to market: Well-defined products and smooth and integrated processes help to create good offers fast.
- Less cost: Costs are reduced due to this reduced time, but also due to reduced product complexity, which is based on standardization and modularization and also allows for more automation.
- Increased customer loyalty: Trust induced by the first three benefits and less mass confusion due to explanations and selected recommendations increase customer loyalty.

---

[5] However, care must be taken to avoid mass confusion, i.e., overwhelming customers with a too large number of decisions they must take.

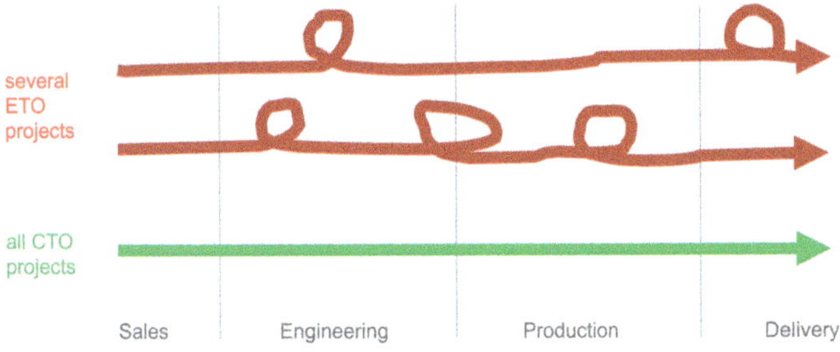


**Fig. 1.5**  Schematic overview of CTO and ETO processes (*Source* Own work)

These are not only general and abstract statements: Configurator vendors and many of their customers have reported concrete numbers (e.g., percentages) of their improvements over previous solutions.

## *Success Stories from the Industry*

Hvam et al. [15] present a case study of a huge industrial product: a cement factory. The study stems from 2008 and reports about only one project at the Danish company FLSmidth, but its findings are still valid today. A cement factory costs 40–140 million EUR and designing and building takes two to three years. As it took the company five weeks to answer a request for proposal, they couldn't even answer half of the inquiries for budgetary offers. They wanted to improve on this and introduced a CTO process: First, they concentrated only on the main properties of the whole factory and the main variants and created a detailed offer based on this. It cost them 800 thousand EUR to build the configurator and it was maintained for 100 thousand EUR per year. Already in the first year of operations, the offers they could submit increased significantly, from 2.700 to 4.500 million EUR (i.e., 70% more opportunities). And 400 million EUR materialized as additional orders. This means 1 million EUR invested in the configurator achieved 400 million EUR more business volume (not revenue). They increased the quality and could reduce the lead time to two days (already the first of three steps reduced the effort for creating offers to 50%).

There are lots of similar success stories for all sizes of product families and enterprises in different industrial sectors: Already in 1989, the development and deployment of a configuration system in a company for computer networks resulted in a net return of more than 40 million USD per year [9]. A configurator for telecommunication systems in 1998 paid off in the first year [6]. In 2002, a seller of electronic switch-boards reduced lead time for offers from 3–4 days to 10 min [16]. A manufacturer of windows and doors achieved a maximum of three weeks from order to delivery in 2008 (instead of 2 months average in industry) [10, 14]. More recently (2022), a German configurator vendor reported in a press release that with their CPQ solution an Austrian company which builds machines could reduce their lead time of offers to the half [26].

Marketing material and sales presentations of the configurator vendors and reports of consulting companies give concrete numbers based on evaluations and customer surveys. Even though those numbers show the realistic potential of CPQ systems, they must be taken with care. Most of them are anecdotal data based on internal evaluations of vendors. Typically, they are published in marketing information or presentations at business conferences, fairs, or customer days, not in scientific publications. Therefore, the threats to validity are unknown. There is a risk that those benefits cannot be achieved by an arbitrary configurator project.

Instead of reproducing such numbers here, we summarize benefits reported by several configurator vendors in such marketing materials:

- 30–40% faster generation of quotes (i.e., improved sales productivity),
- 40–60% reduced errors in quotes and orders,
- 5–15% increase in win rates/sales,
- 1–2% increase in margins.

## Example

Let us introduce a configurable product that will serve as our running example throughout the book: A folding bike. A folding bike is a bicycle that can be easily made more compact by folding it, so it can be transported (e.g., on public transport) like a piece of luggage (cf. Fig. 1.6). One typical customer requirement is that it should be light enough to be carried by hand. We will get to know more constraints along the way.

A UML class diagram[6] [20] for a basic version of the configurable product with some variability is shown in Fig. 1.7. We focus on selected key components for now and will extend the product later.

A folding bike consists of a frame, a seat, and two wheels. Mudguards may optionally be attached to the frame.

Some of the components have configurable properties: The frame's material can be either steel or titanium. The saddle's material can be either synthetic or leather. The seatpost can have one of three types (standard, extended, telescope) to allow for different heights. Each of the wheels may have reflectors or not.
Summing up:

- The product is a folding bike.
- The product family consists of variants with different types and different materials. Its size is 96, calculated by multiplying 4 frame variants (2 materials, each with or without mudguards), 6 seat variants (2 materials, 3 seatposts), and 4 wheel variants (2 times 2 variants with or without reflectors).

---

[6] See the Modeling Notation in Sect. 4.2 if you are not familiar with the UML class diagram notation.

**Fig. 1.6** Folding bike (*Source* istockphoto.com)

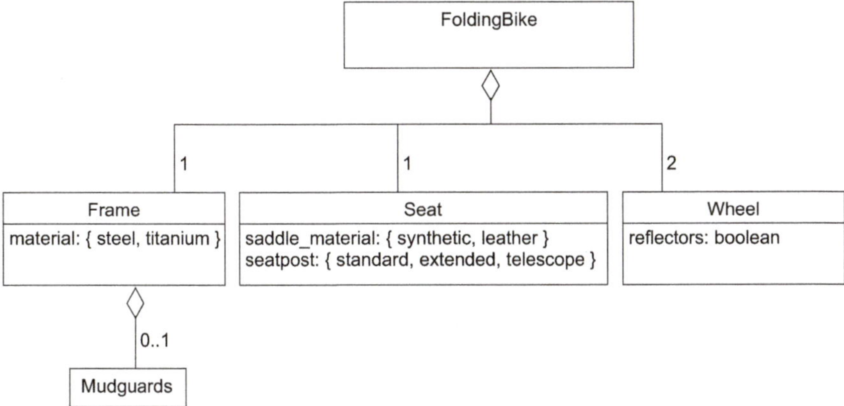


**Fig. 1.7** A basic UML class diagram for folding bikes with some variability (*Source* Own work)

- The production approach is between ATO and CTO because the final bike will most probably be assembled from prefabricated components and only a few restrictions (constraints) need to be taken into account.
- The specification of the product manager may be similar to the description above, whereas the formal representation (by the knowledge engineer) could be similar to the UML diagram. Of course, much more detail[7] would be necessary in practice, e.g., all components have a specified weight and the total weight of the complete bike is the sum of the weights of all selected components.
- The configurator user might be an end-customer. They need a user interface to enter their requirements, e.g., the maximal accepted weight. The solver will ensure that the resulting product complies with this customer requirement by continuously comparing that maximum with the current total weight of the bike.

---

[7] See Chap. 4.

## Exercises

**Exercise 1.1** Pick an interesting example from Cyledge's Configurator Database.[8] Play with it and answer the following questions:

- What is the product?
- What is the variability and complexity (restrictions)?
- What is the benefit (of the configurator) for the buyer (customer)?
- What is annoying (for you as a user)?
- Is the customer's time well spent?

**Exercise 1.2** Assign each of the products in the following list to a production approach (PTO, ATO, CTO, CTO+, ETO) and explain your selection:

- ball-point pen
- entry door
- gas turbine
- railroad interlocking system
- motor bike
- racing car

**Exercise 1.3** What could be stakeholder (even in a wider context) types and responsibilities for the folding bike example?

**Exercise 1.4** What benefits can a folding bike manufacturer achieve when they migrate from mass production to mass customization?

## References


1. Batchelor, J., Andersen, H.R.: Bridging the product configuration gap between PLM and ERP–an automotive case study. In: 19th International Product Development Management Conference, Manchester, UK, pp. 17–19 (2012)
2. Bauernhansl, T., Ten Hompel, M., Vogel-Heuser, B. (eds.): Industrie 4.0 in Produktion, Automatisierung und Logistik: Anwendung. Technologien. Migration. Springer Fachmedien Wiesbaden, Wiesbaden (2014). https://doi.org/10.1007/978-3-658-04682-8
3. Blecker, T., Abdelkafi, N.: Complexity and variety in mass customization systems: analysis and recommendations. Manag. Dec. **44** (2006). https://doi.org/10.1108/00251740610680596
4. Davis, S.M.: Future Perfect. Addison-Wesley (1987)
5. Dell, M., Fredman, C.: Direct from Dell: Strategies that Revolutionized an Industry. HarperBusiness (1999)
6. Fleischanderl, G., Friedrich, G., Haselböck, A., Schreiner, H., Stumptner, M.: Configuring large systems using generative constraint satisfaction. IEEE Intell. Syst. **13**(4), 59–68 (1998). https://doi.org/10.1109/5254.708434
7. Ford, H., Crowther, S.: My Life and Work. Doubleday, Page & Company (1923)


---

[8] https://www.configurator-database.com/

8. Gutiérrez-Fernández, A.M., Chacón-Luna, A.E., Benavides, D., Fuentes, L., Rabiser, R.: Variability management and software product line knowledge in software companies. J. Syst. Softw. **216** (2024). https://doi.org/10.1016/j.jss.2024.112114

9. Harmon, P.: Digital equipment corp. Saves millions with expert systems. Expert Syst. Strat. **3**(8) (1987). https://stacks.stanford.edu/file/druid:rk795nw8403/rk795nw8403.pdf

10. Haug, A., Hvam, L., Mortensen, N.H.: The impact of product configurators on lead times in engineering-oriented companies. Artif. Intell. Eng. Des. Anal. Manuf. **25**(2), 197–206 (2011). https://doi.org/10.1017/S0890060410000636

11. Haug, A., Shafiee, S., Hvam, L.: The costs and benefits of product configuration projects in engineer-to-order companies. Comput. Ind. **105**, 133–142 (2019). https://doi.org/10.1016/J.COMPIND.2018.11.005

12. Hayes, R.H., Wheelwright, S.C.: The dynamics of process-product life cycle. Harvard Bus. Rev. (1979). https://hbr.org/1979/03/the-dynamics-of-process-product-life-cycles

13. Heiskala, M., Tihonen, J., Paloheimo, K.S., Soininen, T.: Mass customization with configurable products and configurators: a review of benefits and challenges. Mass customization information systems in business pp. 1–32 (2007)

14. Hong, G., Hu, L., Xue, D., Tu, Y.L., Xiong, Y.L.: Identification of the optimal product configuration and parameters based on individual customer requirements on performance and costs in one-of-a-kind production. Int. J. Prod. Res. **46**(12), 3297–3326 (2008). https://doi.org/10.1080/00207540601099274

15. Hvam, L., Mortensen, N.H., Riis, J.: Product Customization. Springer (2008)

16. Hvam, L., Riis, J., Malis, M.: A multi-perspective approach for the design of configuration systems. In: Proceedings of the ECAI 2002 Workshop on Configuration, pp. 56–62 (2002)

17. Kha, L.: Critical success factors for business-to-consumer e-business: Lessons from Amazon and Dell. Master's thesis, Massachusetts Institute of Technology (2000)

18. Meinicke, J., Thüm, T., Schröter, R., Benduhn, F., Leich, T., Saake, G.: Mastering Software Variability with FeatureIDE. Springer (2017). https://doi.org/10.1007/978-3-319-61443-4

19. Nordin, A., Motte, D., Hopf, A., Bjärnemo, R., Eckhardt, C.C.: Constraint-handling techniques for generative product design systems in the mass customization context. Artif. Intell. Eng. Des. Anal. Manuf. **27**(4), 387–399 (2013). https://doi.org/10.1017/S0890060413000383

20. Object Management Group: Unified Modeling Language 2.5.1, section 11.4, Classes (2017). https://www.omg.org/spec/UML/2.5.1

21. Piller, F.: Mass Customization. Gabler Verlag, Wiesbaden (2006). https://doi.org/10.1007/978-3-8350-9204-4

22. Pine, J.: Mass Customization: The New Frontier in Business Competition. Harvard Business School Press, Boston, Mass (1993)

23. Raben, C.H.: A product rationalization project part of a portfolio optimization program (2018). http://wiki.doing-projects.org/index.php/A_product_rationalization_project_part_of_a_portfolio_optimization_program

24. Rock, G., Theis, K., Wischnewski, P.: Variability management. In: Stjepandić, J., Wognum, N., Verhagen, W.J.C. (eds.) Concurrent Engineering in the 21st Century: Foundations, Developments and Challenges, pp. 491–519. Springer International Publishing, Cham (2015). https://doi.org/10.1007/978-3-319-13776-6_17

25. Sabin, D., Weigel, R.: Product configuration frameworks - a survey. IEEE Intell. Syst. **13**(4), 42–49 (1998). https://doi.org/10.1109/5254.708432

26. Schröder, S., Dietze, U.: Interview: Industriegüter-Vertrieb im Wandel (2021). https://www.encoway.de/blog/industriegueter-vertrieb-im-wandel/

27. Toffler, A.: Future Shock. Random House (1970)

28. Zhang, L.: Product configuration: a review of the state-of-the-art and future research. Int. J. Prod. Res. **52**, 6381–6398 (2014). https://doi.org/10.1080/00207543.2014.942012

**Open Access**  This chapter is licensed under the terms of the Creative Commons Attribution-NonCommercial-NoDerivatives 4.0 International License (http://creativecommons.org/licenses/by-nc-nd/4.0/), which permits any noncommercial use, sharing, distribution and reproduction in any medium or format, as long as you give appropriate credit to the original author(s) and the source, provide a link to the Creative Commons license and indicate if you modified the licensed material. You do not have permission under this license to share adapted material derived from this chapter or parts of it.

The images or other third party material in this chapter are included in the chapter's Creative Commons license, unless indicated otherwise in a credit line to the material. If material is not included in the chapter's Creative Commons license and your intended use is not permitted by statutory regulation or exceeds the permitted use, you will need to obtain permission directly from the copyright holder.

# Chapter 2
# Scope of Product Configuration

**Abstract** Configurable products have customizable parts (components) and properties (features) with rules (constraints) to ensure technical feasibility and quality. They come in many kinds: physical (hardware) or intangible (software, services), small (e.g., pen) or large (e.g., power plant), simple (e.g., pizza) or complicated (e.g., production schedule), components (e.g., power supply) or systems (e.g., railway interlocking and control), for consumers (e.g., mountain bike) or business (e.g., container ship). Configurators are useful throughout the whole product lifecycle, from pre-sales to service, and have different focus areas in different phases.
This chapter defines the meaning of the terms product and configuration. It shows how variety can be specified by means of concepts such as part-of hierarchy and kind-of hierarchy in a configurable industrial product and an extension of our folding bike example. And it gives an overview over various kinds of configurable products and over different classes of configuration systems.

The term "Product Configuration" consists of two words which nicely span the whole bandwidth of our topic: the product defines the content and is the result to be achieved, while the configuration is the corresponding process. The combination of both implies that the product is not just picked but configured in some way. In the next section we take a closer look at those aspects.

## 2.1 Products and Their Configuration

A product is an artifact in the physical world that is built (by a producer) and bought (by a consumer[1]). Building such a product requires a specification of its structure and materials, often called BOM (Bill Of Materials) [1, 2]. Buying such a product requires a catalogue of the offering, e.g., a list of the available products like in the

---

[1] In a wider sense: a private person as an end-user, or a company which uses it directly for themselves or as a component of products which they sell.

© Siemens Aktiengesellschaft Österreich 2026

R. Comploi-Taupe and A. Falkner, *Product Configuration*,
SpringerBriefs in Computer Science,
https://doi.org/10.1007/978-3-032-17163-4_2

era of mass production, with dozens or hundreds of similar variants distinguished by the main discriminating properties. For larger and/or richer products this can easily explode to thousands or millions of variants which can no longer be explicitly listed. Here, configurability comes in: the buyer does not select a complete product, but preferred values for a set of product properties. Those span implicitly the whole variety of a product. To be exact, "product" does not directly mean the physical artifact here, but a specification for it—often called "product family" [7] or "product line".[2] Summarizing, the definition of the variety of such a configurable product typically comprises [13]:

- component types and structure (part tree)
- properties (parameters with various domains)
- restrictions (constraints) on components and properties.

Configuration in the stricter sense is the process (task) to find those combinations of components that fulfill all customer needs [12].[3] It covers the following goals [8]:

- help a user to fulfill all (or at least most) customer requirements
- avoid offering incompatible or inefficient combinations of components and/or properties
- optionally, optimize (or rank) the results w.r.t. given objectives.

## 2.2  Modeling the Product Structure

For configurable products it is important to have a common product structure, i.e., some kind of system architecture or part-of hierarchy, which is the skeleton for the variety of the subparts (i.e., the possible types of components). Figure 2.1 sketches this approach to specify a product family, which is sometimes called "Product Variant Master" [6] and comprises a Part-of structure (Architecture) and a Kind-of hierarchy (Variants).[4]

In that example, we see a product family of hardware racks, which comprise one or two frames and a power supply [3]. As each frame can comprise a certain number of modules, the part-of hierarchy forms a tree structure which is typical for most configurable products. The potential number of modules for a frame is bounded by nine (six in the upper row, and three in the lower row)—a number which can of course be much higher in the real world.

The kind-of hierarchy is flat and untypically small in that example. Frames come in two types: two rows or only one row (with a mandatory module in the left-most

---

[2] In practice, the term "product" is used for both the physical artifact, which can be owned, and the specification of it—an instance of the product family—which is configured and ordered.

[3] Often, the term "configuration" is also used for the result of the configuration process, i.e., a product configuration is the resulting product instance after the configuration.

[4] A similar but more powerful representation is introduced in Chap. 4.

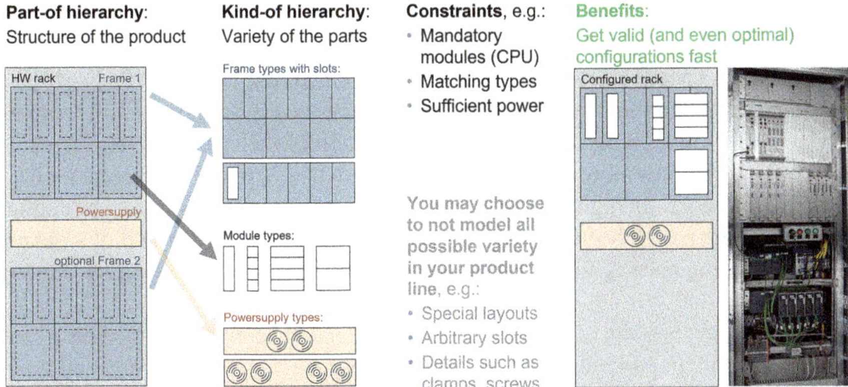



**Fig. 2.1** Taming product variety by product line specification (*Photo source* Leaflet "Trackguard Sicas S7 electronic interlocking" © Siemens AG 2014)

position). There are four module types, two for each slot width (narrow or wide) in the frame. And there are two types of power supply. One can easily calculate that this leads to thousands of different products.[5]

Often, certain combinations of part types are not allowed in the structure. Some of such constraints were already mentioned above: e.g., module types must match slot width. Others could be that a weak power supply does not work for two frames, or that each frame requires a certain module (e.g., a CPU).

A configuration process [4] starts with the user taking a decision, e.g., selecting a two-row frame in the upper part of the rack, and none in the lower. This allows the configurator to suggest the weak power supply. According to the customer requirements, the user will proceed with placing the modules. And each decision may cause some potential values for the remaining decisions to be filtered away due to the constraints. On user request, the configurator can auto-complete the configuration to fulfill all requirements in an optimal way. At the end, the customer will have a full configuration where all selections are valid and efficient.

To ensure performance of the configurator and keep development costs reasonable, not all details or specialities shall be modelled. In fact, a model is always a reduction of the reality which concentrates on the important aspects.

## 2.3 Types of Products

Which types of products are subject to configuration? What comes first to mind are the typical consumer products such as cars, computers, shirts, etc. All of them are physical products and have—due to their relatively small and therefore manageable

---

[5] Cf. Chap. 5 on how to calculate the variety.

complexity—a certain relationship with mass production. They are a main scope of the field of mass customization which also covers production processes and how they can be tuned to achieve an efficient fulfilment of customized orders [10, 11, 14].

Product configuration has a much wider focus and covers larger and more complex products, also for B2B customers. The configuration of such products (e.g., a whole power plant) requires more expressive specification languages and elaborate tooling.

And even more, intangible products such as software and services can be configured in a similar way. Software systems are the main scope of the field of software product line engineering which helps to ensure the quality of the result by running tests [5].

Summing up, product configuration in general and the corresponding tools by the various vendors in particular offer technologies which are appropriate for all types of products such as listed below.

Physical products:

- Consumer products: cars, computers, clothes, doors, etc.
- Industrial products: compressors, turbines, engines, x-ray detectors, etc.
- Complex systems: telephone switches, railway interlockings, cement factories, emergency room equipment, etc.

Intangible products:

- Software systems: operating system configuration, traffic control, etc.
- Services: computer networks, power providers, long-term maintenance contracts, installation services, etc.
- Consumer contracts: insurances, media subscriptions, holiday plans, etc.
- Plans: project plans, production schedules, bills of processes (BOP), etc.

## 2.4  Configurator Types in the Product Lifecycle

Configuration systems cover not only a wide variety of products, but also a wide variety of the whole product lifecycle from product management over sales, order processing, engineering, and production to service and maintenance. In all these phases, product configuration helps and can be used as a database for transferring information from one of these business processes to the next. Figure 2.2 shows that we can roughly distinguish five classes of configurators: For pre-sales configurators it is important to inform customers of the quality of the product and its outstanding features, to give a recommendation, and even approximate price calculations or alternatives. The typical sales configurator or CPQ system must have a high usability (a kind of guided selling), as it will be very often used by the customer themself. Engineering configurators go into much more details to ensure consistency of a technical product as well as accuracy of the calculations which is especially important to get a well-based offer for complex systems, and very often sales personnel will

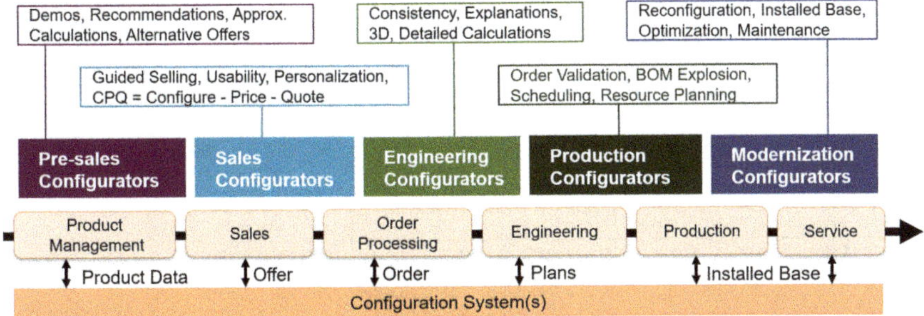


**Fig. 2.2** Configurators serve the whole product lifecycle (*Source* Own work)

be the typical users. As production configurators take the production capabilities of the factory into account, they include order validation, materials, bill of materials, scheduling, and resource planning. Once the product is in use, e.g., a huge system such as a steel plant, there is the issue of modernization, e.g., complying with new regulations by the authorities, like decarbonization. There it is important to know what is installed and help the operators to optimally reconfigure their systems to make them more efficient and, e.g., reduce their environmental footprint.

## Example

We revisit the folding bike example from Chap. 1 and extend it in Fig. 2.3. An electric folding bike is a special case of a folding bike, it additionally contains a motor and a battery.

Figures 2.4 and 2.5 depict UML object diagrams [9] representing two variants of this configurable product.

## Exercises

**Exercise 2.1** Browse through Cyledge's Configurator Database[6] to get a feeling for the scope of configurable products. How deep and wide are their part-of and kind-of hierarchies?

**Exercise 2.2** How many variants are there for the configurable product in Fig. 1.7, and how many for the one in Fig. 2.3?

---

[6] https://www.configurator-database.com/.

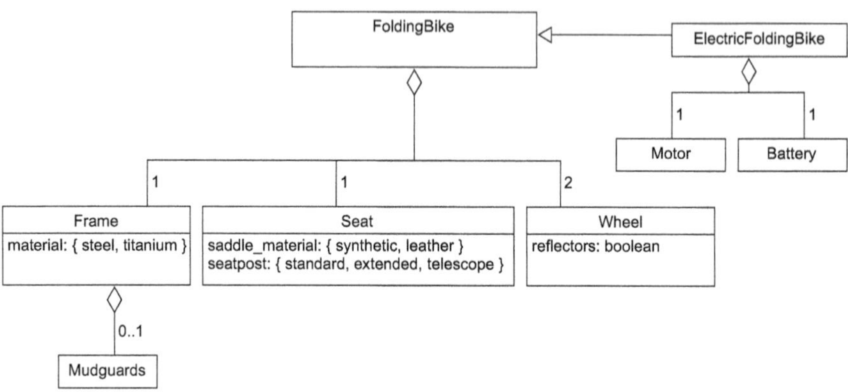


**Fig. 2.3**  The UML class diagram for folding bikes from Fig. 1.7, extended by a specialization for electric bikes (*Source* Own work)

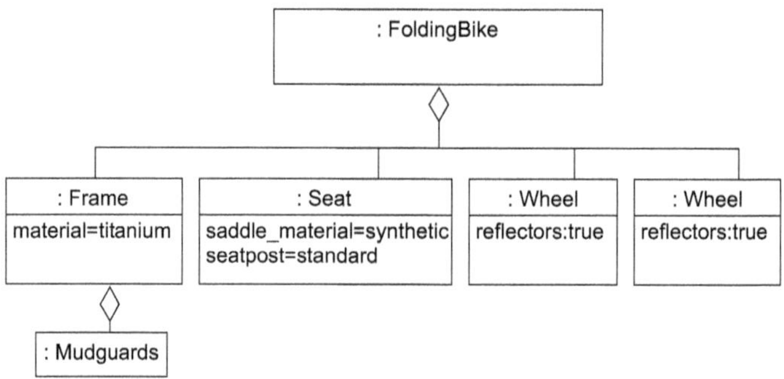


**Fig. 2.4**  An UML object diagram showing one variant of the configurable folding bike (*Source* Own work)

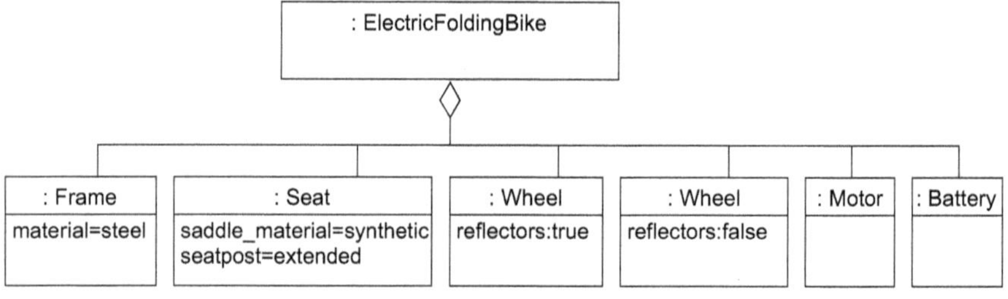


**Fig. 2.5**  An UML object diagram showing another variant of the configurable folding bike (*Source* Own work)

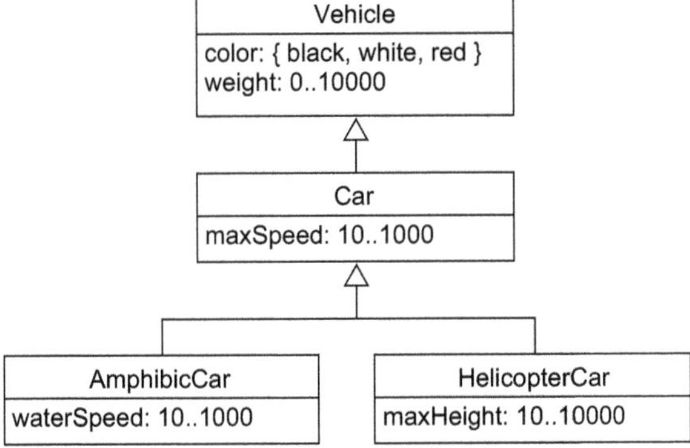

**Fig. 2.6** A basic UML class diagram for some variants of cars (*Source* Own work)



**Exercise 2.3** How many variants are there in the hardware racks example in Fig. 2.1 (considering just the part-of hierarchy and kind-of hierarchy without additional constraints)? Document any assumptions you make for your estimation. Justify your answer by a transparent calculation.

**Exercise 2.4** Continuing from Exercise 2.3: How would the number of variants behave with increasing number of frames?

**Exercise 2.5** A car manufacturer decided to model their offering with a kind-of hierarchy comprising root class `Vehicle` (with properties `color` and `weight`) and sub-class `Car` (with property `maxSpeed`). When they introduced amphibic cars, they added sub-sub-class `AmphibicCar` (with property `waterSpeed`) to the hierarchy. When they introduced air-borne cars, they added sub-sub-class `HelicopterCar` (with property `maxHeight`) to the hierarchy—see Fig. 2.6.

Now they want to offer air-borne amphibic cars. How can they adapt their model? Is a part-of hierarchy an appropriate alternative?

# References


1. Blumöhr, U., Münch, M., Ukalovic, M.: Variant Configuration with SAP, 2nd edn. SAP PRESS (2011)
2. Dhungana, D., Falkner, A.A., Haselböck, A., Taupe, R.: Enabling integrated product and factory configuration in smart production ecosystems. In: 43rd Euromicro Conference on Software Engineering and Advanced Applications, SEAA 2017, Vienna, Austria, August 30 - Sept. 1, 2017, pp. 266–273. IEEE Computer Society (2017). https://doi.org/10.1109/SEAA.2017.26
3. Falkner, A.A., Friedrich, G., Haselböck, A., Schenner, G., Schreiner, H.: Twenty-five years of successful application of constraint technologies at Siemens. AI Mag. **37**(4), 67–80 (2016). https://doi.org/10.1609/AIMAG.V37I4.2688
4. Falkner, A.A., Haselböck, A., Krames, G., Schenner, G., Schreiner, H., Taupe, R.: Solver requirements for interactive configuration. J. Univers. Comput. Sci. **26**(3), 343–373 (2020). http://www.jucs.org/jucs_26_3/solver_requirements_for_interactive

5. Felfernig, A., Falkner, A., Benavides, D.: Feature Models: AI-Driven Design, Analysis and Applications. SpringerBriefs in Computer Science. Springer International Publishing, Cham (2024). https://doi.org/10.1007/978-3-031-61874-1
6. Hvam, L., Mortensen, N.H., Riis, J.: Product Customization. Springer (2008)
7. Jiao, J., Tseng, M.M.: A methodology of developing product family architecture for mass customization. J. Intell. Manuf. **10**(1), 3–20 (1999). https://doi.org/10.1023/A:1008926428533
8. Junker, U.: Configuration. In: Rossi, F., van Beek, P., Walsh, T. (eds.) Handbook of Constraint Programming, pp. 837–873. Elsevier Science (2006)
9. Object Management Group: Unified Modeling Language 2.5.1, section 9.8, Instances (2017). https://www.omg.org/spec/UML/2.5.1
10. Piller, F.: Mass Customization. Gabler Verlag, Wiesbaden (2006). https://doi.org/10.1007/978-3-8350-9204-4
11. Piller, F.T.: Mass customization: reflections on the state of the concept. Int. J. Flex. Manuf. Syst. **16**(4), 313–334 (2004). https://doi.org/10.1007/s10696-005-5170-x
12. Sabin, D., Weigel, R.: Product configuration frameworks - a survey. IEEE Intell. Syst. **13**(4), 42–49 (1998). https://doi.org/10.1109/5254.708432
13. Soininen, T., Tiihonen, J., Männistö, T., Sulonen, R.: Towards a general ontology of configuration. Artif. Intell. Eng. Des. Anal. Manuf. **12**(4), 357–372 (1998). http://journals.cambridge.org/action/displayAbstract?aid=38651
14. Tseng, M.M., Jiao, J.: Mass customization. In: Salvendy, G. (ed.) Handbook of Industrial Engineering, pp. 684–709. Wiley (2001). https://doi.org/10.1002/9780470172339.ch25

**Open Access** This chapter is licensed under the terms of the Creative Commons Attribution-NonCommercial-NoDerivatives 4.0 International License (http://creativecommons.org/licenses/by-nc-nd/4.0/), which permits any noncommercial use, sharing, distribution and reproduction in any medium or format, as long as you give appropriate credit to the original author(s) and the source, provide a link to the Creative Commons license and indicate if you modified the licensed material. You do not have permission under this license to share adapted material derived from this chapter or parts of it.

The images or other third party material in this chapter are included in the chapter's Creative Commons license, unless indicated otherwise in a credit line to the material. If material is not included in the chapter's Creative Commons license and your intended use is not permitted by statutory regulation or exceeds the permitted use, you will need to obtain permission directly from the copyright holder.

# Chapter 3
# Business Context and Architectures

**Abstract** Product configuration connects to other business processes such as Customer Relationship Management, Product Lifecycle Management, Supply Chain Management, and Enterprise Resource Planning. Configuration Lifecycle Management can serve as a single source of truth that ties together all product knowledge relevant to configuration. A good architecture is based on proven concepts such as defined data storage, standard interfaces, clear responsibilities (services), separation of concerns (modularity), and flexibility to adapt to changing requirements and environments. In this chapter, we introduce different views on the same configurable product that support the integration of product configuration into the broader business ecosystem. We discuss system architecture considerations and data integration aspects, providing practical guidance for implementing configuration systems in real-world environments.

Product configuration does not stand alone; rather, it is connected, even intertwined, with other tasks. It relies on knowledge of customer requirements (i.e., eliciting and understanding them) as well as detailed information about available product data and functionality. To fulfill a customer order, production capabilities need to be taken into account. And of course, all of this depends on the IT landscape in place. Figure 3.1 provides an overview of the entire context.

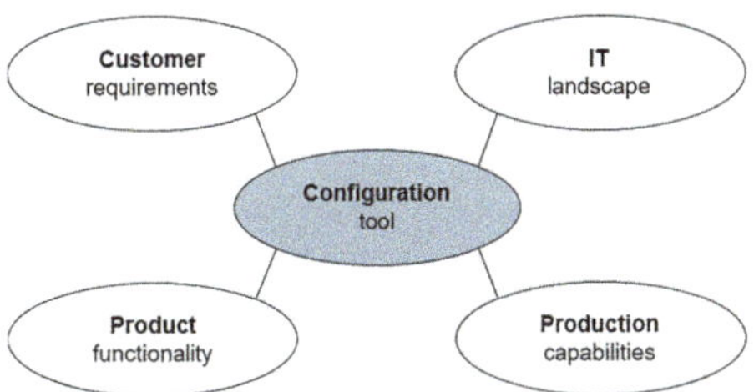


**Fig. 3.1** Overview of the product configuration context (*Source* Own work)

© Siemens Aktiengesellschaft Österreich 2026

R. Comploi-Taupe and A. Falkner, *Product Configuration*,
SpringerBriefs in Computer Science,
https://doi.org/10.1007/978-3-032-17163-4_3

## 3.1 Related Business Processes

Figure 3.2 shows the corresponding business processes and, on the left-hand side, the typical situation in many existing systems where configuration logic is authored and maintained in separate tools (represented by circles): Customer Relationship Management (CRM) covers all interactions with customers, from marketing, offering, and sales, to customer data and tracking [14]. Product Lifecycle Management (PLM) comprises the definition of product data, from product design (ensuring functionality and feasibility) to manufacturing, service, and disposal [20]. Enterprise Resource Planning (ERP) [13] and Supply Chain Management (SCM) [19] focus on the realization, i.e., the flow of concrete materials and assemblies through the production of the complete product by concrete machines. Roughly, it is a flow from product development on the left to operations on the right. There might also be other special legacy systems, and all these tools implement part of the configuration logic and typically overlap. Even for well-maintained systems, this has consequences one would like to avoid:

- Redundant code
- Multiple maintenance efforts
- Misaligned data
- Lack of overview
- Suboptimal planning
- Inefficient propagation of changes.

To mitigate these problems, we could use one of the involved tools as a controller for configuration logic. However, it does not fit well into product development alone, because the latter has a project-like, time-to-market focus, and product data typically change more often than customer requirements. On the other hand, it does not fit well into operations either, because the latter is transaction-based and has a high

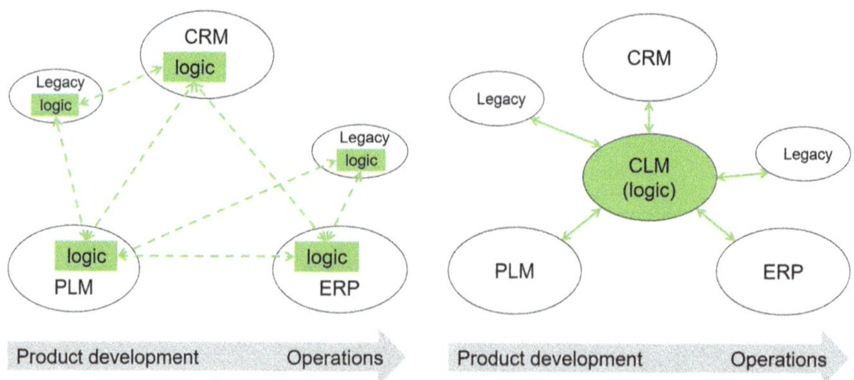


**Fig. 3.2** Configuration Lifecycle Management aligns all product knowledge (*Source* Own work, inspired by [22])

customer focus that relies on stable product data. Nevertheless, vendors of PLM, CRM, and ERP systems are aware of these problems and try to cover configuration logic themselves. For example, both Salesforce (CRM) [16] and SAP (ERP) [7] have configurators that can exploit the respective focus of their systems but do not achieve the generality of dedicated configuration systems. Siemens' Teamcenter (PLM) [4] can integrate its configurators (from ATO to ETO) with its product design, where it is very strong. Thus, it offers a backbone for variability, meaning that it has all the product and configuration knowledge in its system and connects it to the sales platform and manufacturing.

## 3.2 Configuration Lifecycle Management

Some vendors of configuration systems favor a Configuration Lifecycle Management (CLM) approach. This term was introduced in 2012 by one of the leading configurator companies, Configit [3]. CLM aims to combine all data relevant to configuration in one place (the CLM tool) and to share it with all other systems (as sketched on the right-hand side of Fig. 3.2). This single source of truth with respect to configuration serves as a complete, correct, and always up-to-date central database and offers the following advantages:

- Aligned configuration data,
- cross-area overview,
- controlled release process for changes,
- an integrated link between product development and operations,
- enterprise-wide access to configuration definitions, and
- a collaboration tool for configurations.

Such an approach fosters the inclusion of all phases of the product lifecycle (including production, maintenance, and service) in the decisions during the configuration process. Their effects can be anticipated and balanced; for example, planning for a circular economy can be done already at the point of sale. We will cover this aspect in more detail in Chap. 9.

The user interface (and the underlying logic) of CLM-based configurators typically represents all its data in a chain of views that is ordered in terms of proximity and importance to the customer, which also implies a temporal order. This chain of views is shown from top to bottom in Fig. 3.3. It starts with comparatively little data (customer requirements and options of the offering) in the sales view, which is the focus of CRM. Then we have the engineering view, which defines the feasible product structure and variety and is based upon PLM data. This is followed by the parts view (often hidden from the customer), which relies on ERP data and selects the available materials that optimally implement the configured product according to known non-functional requirements such as cost, sustainability, etc. At the end, we have the production view, which is about scheduling and perhaps takes into account

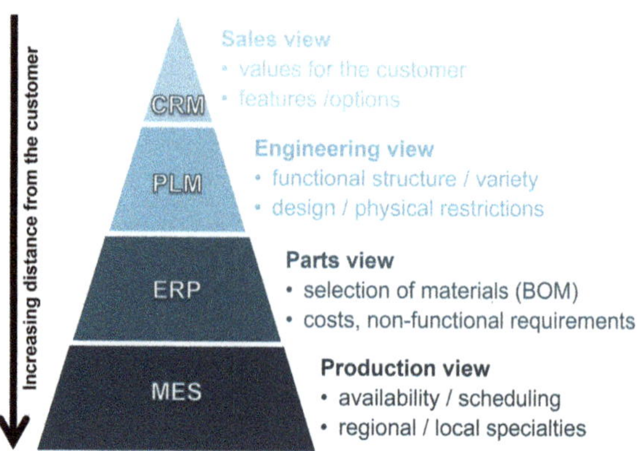



**Fig. 3.3** From sales to production (*Source* Own work)

regional and local availabilities. It is connected to the Manufacturing Execution System (MES).

## 3.3  Architectural Aspects to Consider

There are numerous vendors of commercial configuration tools, coming either as part of one of the related business processes (CRM, PLM, ERP, etc.) or as a separate application, and all of them have different strengths and weaknesses (see Sect. 5.6 for some examples).

The temptation is significant to pick one of these commercial vendors (hopefully after a thorough evaluation and proof-of-concept, cf. Sect. 7.3) and let their experts (help) set up the basic architecture and implement and roll out the first configurator versions. This is reasonable because they know their tool and typically have sufficient experience from previous installations at other customers.

However, this may lead to a monolithic and proprietary solution that, on the one hand, fits more to the capabilities of the vendor's tool than to the buyer's real requirements, and, on the other hand, bears a high risk of vendor lock-in. Vendor lock-in means that migration to another tool is practically impossible due to technical difficulties and high costs. Technical difficulties are related to fundamentally diverse approaches and the tendency of (some) vendors to keep their model representation private; for example, by offering only cloud-based modeling environments without public file importers and exporters. Migration costs can reach a level near re-implementation from scratch, but a migration may easily become necessary because the vendor either unfairly increases prices or falls significantly behind competitors in terms of technology.

Therefore, it is always worth considering a more open and flexible architecture, even if it requires better-trained experts within the company. Especially if the company has an IT department, architects, solution designers, and DevOps experts may

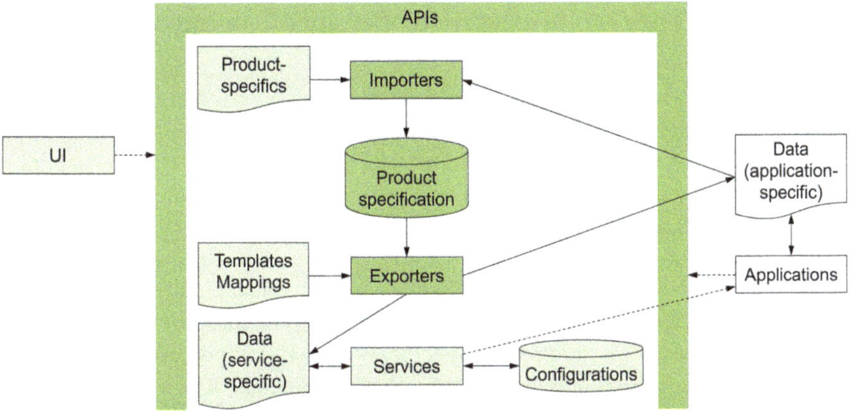


**Fig. 3.4** Reference architecture for product configuration (*Source* Own work)

already be available—and they will know all the best practices and conventions for software within the company, for example, concerning regulations, standards, security, etc.

Some companies favor a dataflow approach: Product data move through several stations and are adapted and/or extended along the way; for example, combining customer requirements and technical product specifications results in a first version of the configured product, which is later refined based on part availabilities from the ERP system, pricing information leads to further adaptations, etc. Such an approach works well for straightforward processes, but less so for iterative processes with various cycles of varying lengths. In practice, cycles will occur often; for example, due to customer feedback, supply chain issues, or incremental enhancements of the installed product. We believe that a classical architecture, as sketched in Fig. 3.4 or Fig. 4.2, can deal better with such a situation.

A comprehensive configuration system architecture in a classical service-oriented style must comprise:

- Data storage for all relevant data (product specification, suppliers, costs and prices, customer requirements, etc.): database or knowledge graph as a single source of truth
- Interfaces to other systems: import and export to PLM, CRM, ERP, MES, etc.
- APIs (services) for all relevant actions: accessing the data storage, calling the importers and exporters, etc.
- User interfaces for clear and easy interaction with the tool: menus, tables, trees, graphs, but also an LLM-based chatbot (configuration copilot, modeling copilot, agentic framework).[1]

---

[1] See Chap. 8 for more on LLM-based configurator UIs.

## 3.4   A Reference Architecture for Product Configuration

Figure 3.4 shows a generic reference architecture based on these components: We have data storage for the product specification at the center, defined by a configuration modeling language[2] (or ontology). Various importers and exporters translate other notations and formats to and from this content (they are based on the same ontology, which is symbolized by the dark green coloring). Each importer and exporter is generic, i.e., it translates from one format to another without needing to know about the product line content. Product-specific details such as mappings or templates can be supplied by the modeler. Optionally, the data storage also comprises concrete configurations based on the product specification. Services process the content of the product specification and the configurations. Optionally, they can call external applications to accomplish their work. All these components and data are accessible to other applications and user interfaces via APIs. Additionally, the architecture must be able to handle workflows and versions (not explicitly shown in the figure).

A company that wants to set up a concrete configurator architecture for several product families must implement or integrate concrete components for the generic building blocks:

- UIs: Web browser, UML editor, chatbots, etc.
- Data storage: Relational database, RDF triple store, etc.
- Importers and exporters: Microsoft Excel tables, constraint languages (e.g., Mini-Zinc), logic model (e.g., COOM), commercial tools (e.g., SAP, Teamcenter, Tacton), etc.[3]
- Services for modeling: Variability analysis, diagnosis (e.g., unsolvable constraints), table normalization, etc.
- Services for configuration: Consistency check, optimization, etc.

Unfortunately, there are no globally defined and accepted standards—neither for a configuration data model, nor for interfaces, nor for services. However, some companies have achieved a de facto industrial standard due to their significant market presence (e.g., SAP with its model for variant configuration [7]), and some neighboring fields have established standards (e.g., FODA for product line engineering [12], UVL for variability management [5], SysML for systems engineering [10]). Furthermore, vendors realize the benefits of modular solutions and suggest a middleware for configuration [24] (e.g., Configit [9]: "By decoupling the "C" in configure, price and quote solutions, manufacturers can truly scale their operations as products continue to become more complex"). Alternatively, building upon proven patterns and open concepts such as microservices, JSON, UML, RDF, etc., leads to sufficient flexibility and resilience of the architecture.[4]

---

[2] Details for such a notation are described in Chap. 4.

[3] See Sect. 5.6 for more on commercial configurator tools.

[4] See Chap. 8 for one use case for JSON as a representation language for product configuration.

Data storage can benefit from applying semantic web technology (ontologies) to product configuration [1, 2, 11, 17, 18, 23]. CONTO (CONfiguration ONTOlogy and TOols) [6] is an ontology-based semantic framework that supports interoperability between different product configuration systems through a domain-independent, exchangeable semantic configuration model.

## Example

Let us extend the class diagram from Fig. 2.3 in Chap. 2 with more features to illustrate the views introduced in this chapter.

### *PLM/Engineering View*

Figure 3.5 introduces a new class, `RegularFoldingBike`, so that every instance of `FoldingBike` will be an instance of a leaf class (which is a convention sometimes common in product configuration). Most parts of the bike (frame, seat, and wheels) are (still) associated to the root class, so that they are necessary parts of both kinds of bikes. Only for the electric folding bike, additional parts (motor and battery) must be included. Furthermore, we have added role names to some association ends so that we can refer to them (e.g., in constraints). The resulting class diagram is our current PLM/engineering view of the configurable folding bike product.

When modeling a configurable product, it is a good idea to start with the engineering view and thus with a focus on the product itself. Some kind of diagram is usually helpful to visualize the structure. Here, we use UML class diagrams, but other visual languages are also possible.

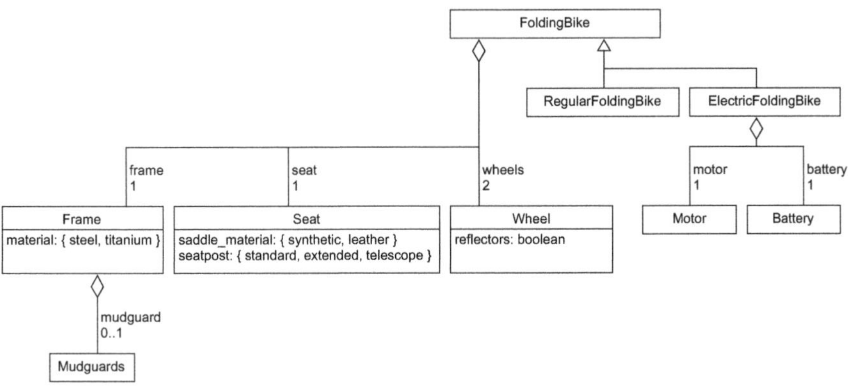


**Fig. 3.5** PLM/Engineering view on the folding bike example (*Source* Own work)

The engineering view furthermore contains the constraint that the two wheels must be configured in the same way. In pseudocode, this may look like this:

$$wheels[1].reflectors = wheels[2].reflectors$$

We recommend formulating constraints in pseudocode because this makes the intention clearer compared to natural language. Constraints should also be shown together with the class diagram, such as Fig. 3.5, so that they can be better understood by its readers. UML class diagrams even support the definition of constraints in a language called Object Constraint Language (OCL) [15, 21].

## *CRM/Sales View*

Figure 3.6 shows the CRM/sales view for the folding bike. It specifies that the customer may specify the following data and requirements:

- the customer's height in centimeters (an integer between 150 and 200),[5]
- whether the bike shall be suitable for off-road usage or not,
- and whether the bike shall be suitable for vegans (i.e., free from animal products).

These requirements are included in the following constraints:

- If the customer's height is less than or equal to 180 cm, the standard seatpost can be chosen.
- If the customer's height is between 177 cm and 189 cm (inclusive), the extended seatpost can be chosen.
- If the customer's height is greater than 185 cm, the telescope seatpost can be chosen.[6]
- If the bike shall be suitable for off-road usage, mudguards shall be included.
- If the bike shall be suitable for vegans, the saddle's material must not be leather.

In pseudocode, the same constraints could be formulated as follows (where "$\Longrightarrow$" stands for logical implication, i.e., "if-then"):

- $customer\_height > 180 \implies seat.seatpost \neq$ "standard"
- $customer\_height \notin 177..189 \implies seat.seatpost \neq$ "extended"
- $customer\_height \leq 185 \implies seat.seatpost \neq$ "telescope"
- $offroad \implies frame.mudguard$ not empty
- $vegan \implies seat.saddle\_material \neq$ "leather"

---

[5] This choice of domain will not be applicable to all customers (cf. https://ourworldindata.org/human-height), but is more than needed for the constraints in our example.

[6] The overlap between the seatpost constraints is there on purpose.

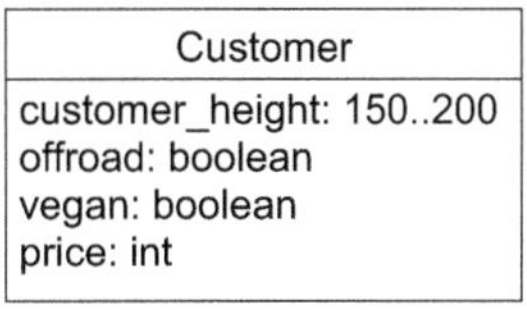

**Fig. 3.6** CRM/Sales view
on the folding bike example
(*Source* Own work)

| Customer |
| --- |
| customer_height: 150..200<br>offroad: boolean<br>vegan: boolean<br>price: int |

In this case, the pseudocode representations of the constraints might be perceived as less readable than the natural-language constraints. The reason is that expressions such as "can be" are actually not constraints: formal constraints have to express what can *not* be (or what *must* be)! Usually, there are several equivalent ways to express the same constraint, and some ways are more understandable than others (but this is also a matter of personal preference). For example, the first three constraints are equivalent to their respective contrapositive:

- $seat.seatpost =$ "standard" $\implies customer\_height \leq 180$
- $seat.seatpost =$ "extended" $\implies customer\_height \in 177..189$
- $seat.seatpost =$ "telescope" $\implies customer\_height > 185$

Furthermore, the CRM/sales view in Fig. 3.6 includes an integer attribute *price* that represents the total price of the product in euro cents. The customer can restrict the price by adding appropriate constraints; for example, that it must be smaller than or equal to a certain upper bound. Other constraints will constrain the value of the *price* attribute to be calculated as the sum of costs of the included parts (i.e., the Bill of Materials (BOM), cf. the ERP/parts view below), plus the sum of manufacturing costs (i.e., the Bill of Processes (BOP)), plus a margin (e.g., 20%).

## *ERP/Parts View*

Figure 3.7 and Table 3.1 show the ERP/parts view for the folding bike.[7] The table (which just shows part of the data for illustration) contains a column with part prices (in euro cents); it could be extended with columns for $CO_2$ footprint, delivery times, etc. The table is greatly simplified. In reality, it would contain many columns to distinguish between component variants. In Table 3.1, the ID values also contain attribute values such as saddle material and seatpost type.[8]

---

[7] The name of the class, *Material*, refers to components/parts offered by various suppliers and must not be confused with the attribute *saddle_material* in our example.

[8] In a real parts table, component variants should be modeled with additional table columns so as not to violate Codd's first normal form [8].

```
┌─────────────────────────┐
│         Material        │
├─────────────────────────┤
│ id: string              │
│ component: string       │
│ supplier: string        │
│ cost: int               │
└─────────────────────────┘
```

**Fig. 3.7** ERP/Parts view on the folding bike example (generic UML class) (*Source* Own work)

**Table 3.1** ERP/Parts view on the folding bike example

| ID | Component | Supplier | Cost |
|---|---|---|---|
| A-Wheel | Wheel | A | 3300 |
| B-Wheel | Wheel | B | 2800 |
| C-Seat-Synthetic-Standard | Seat | C | 5000 |
| C-Seat-Synthetic-Extended | Seat | C | 15000 |
| C-Seat-Synthetic-Telescope | Seat | C | 20000 |
| D-Frame-Steel | Frame | D | 20000 |
| E-Frame-Titanium | Frame | E | 21000 |
| D-Mudguards | Mudguards | D | 3000 |
| D-Motor | Motor | D | 30000 |
| D-Battery | Battery | D | 10000 |
| F-Battery | Battery | F | 9000 |

## *Integrated View*

Figure 3.8 shows an integrated view of the folding bike example that includes the engineering view, the sales view, and the parts view (without constraints and parts table). UML aggregations are used to associate each folding bike "root object" to exactly one set of customer requirements and each component with exactly one material.

## *Configuration Scenario*

Table 3.2 shows an exemplary configuration scenario for the folding bike example, i.e., a series of user interactions and their effects. Initially, when a user starts a configuration session, all options are still available to choose from. In this simplified example, we assume that the user can only enter their height and choose a seatpost, and observe the computed total price.[9] After entering the value 177 cm for the customer's height, the domain of the seatpost variable is reduced according to the constraints. From the remaining options, the user first chooses the extended seatpost.

---

[9] For the other decisions, we assume default values.

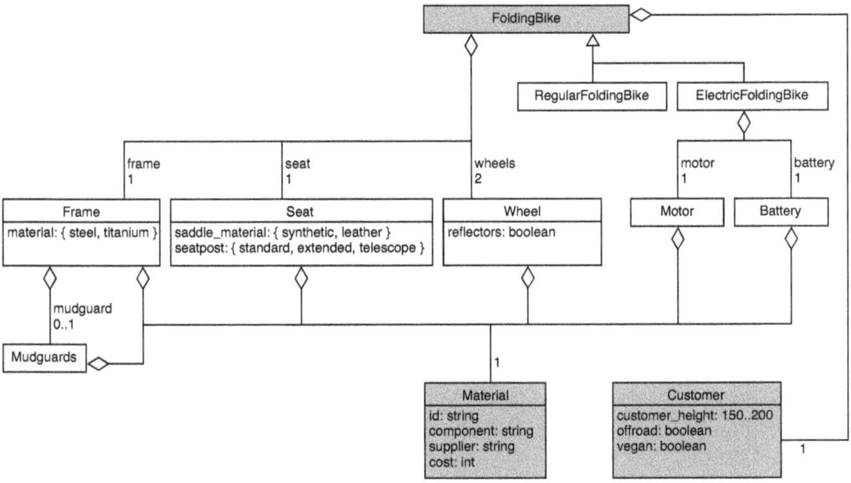

**Fig. 3.8** Integrated view on the folding bike example (without constraints and parts table) (*Source* Own work)

**Table 3.2** Example configuration scenario for the folding bike example (*Source* Own work)

| Action | Customer height | Seatpost | Total price |
|---|---|---|---|
| Start | 150..200 | { standard, extended, telescope } | ? |
| Customer Height = 177 cm | 177 | { standard, extended } | ? |
| Seatpost = extended | 177 | { extended } | €606.- |
| Seatpost = standard | 177 | { standard } | €506.- |

Since the configuration is now complete for the first time, a price can be calculated and shown to the user. Next, the user changes the chosen seatpost to "standard" to see how this changes the total price.[10]

# Exercises

**Exercise 3.1** How many variants (valid configurations) are there for the folding bike when considering only the PLM view in Fig. 3.5 including the constraint on the wheels?

---

[10] The total price of the configured product is calculated in the attribute *Customer*.*price* and larger than the sum of costs of the used materials because it includes manufacturing costs and a margin; see the text on the CRM/Sales View above. Here we used the most economic selection of materials (steel frame, wheels from supplier B—see Table 3.1) and, for simplicity, a constant surcharge of 200 EUR.

**Exercise 3.2** Extend the folding bike example with the customer requirement to support navigation by means of a smartphone. If set to true, the folding bike shall be equipped with a phone mount.

**Exercise 3.3** Extend the folding bike example with the customer requirement to comply with road traffic regulations. If set to true, the folding bike shall be equipped with reflectors, lighting, and a bell (or other features, depending on the selected regulations).

Provide engineering view, sales view, and parts view in the form of UML class diagrams created with UMLet[11] or another adequate tool. Provide a table for the parts view, inventing values that make sense. Provide adequate constraints in pseudocode.

As a possible extension to this exercise, compliance with road traffic regulations may depend on the customer's country and/or bike type (required features may vary from country to country and, for example, there are special regulations for racing bikes in Austria).

**Exercise 3.4** What other customer requirements (and corresponding effects on various views of the products, and constraints) for the folding bike can you think of?

**Exercise 3.5** How can the user experience in the configuration scenario in Table 3.2 be improved?

# References


1. Abbasi, E.K., Leclercq, T., Heymans, P.: A meta-model for product configuration ontologies. In: A. Felfernig, L. Fuentes, J. Cleland-Huang, W.K.G. Assunção, C. Quinton, J. Guo, K. Schmid, M. Huchard, I. Ayala, J.M. Rojas, V. Le, J.M. Horcas (eds.) SPLC '22: 26th ACM International Systems and Software Product Line Conference, Graz, Austria, September 12–16, 2022, Volume B, pp. 166–173. ACM (2022). https://doi.org/10.1145/3503229.3547044
2. Amini, M.M., Coudert, T., Vareilles, É., Aldanondo, M.: Integration of ontologies and constraint satisfaction problems for product configuration. In: IEEE International Conference on Industrial Engineering and Engineering Management, IEEM 2021, Singapore, December 13–16, 2021, pp. 578–582. IEEE (2021). https://doi.org/10.1109/IEEM50564.2021.9672918
3. Batchelor, J., Andersen, H.R.: Bridging the product configuration gap between PLM and ERP - an automotive case study. In: 19th International product development management Conference, Manchester, UK, pp. 17–19 (2012)
4. Bauer, J.: Teamcenter product configurator (2022). https://blogs.sw.siemens.com/teamcenter/cad-clearance-analysis/
5. Benavides, D., Sundermann, C., Feichtinger, K., Galindo, J.A., Rabiser, R., Thüm, T.: UVL: feature modelling with the universal variability language. J. Syst. Softw. **225**, 112326 (2025). https://doi.org/10.1016/J.JSS.2024.112326
6. Bischof, S., Falkner, A., Schneider, P., Steyskal, S., Topa, M.: CONTO: An ontology-based approach for interoperable configuration knowledge. In: SEMANTiCS'25: International Conference on Semantic Systems (2025)
7. Blumöhr, U., Münch, M., Ukalovic, M.: Variant Configuration with SAP, 2nd edn. SAP PRESS (2011)


---

[11] https://www.umlet.com/.

8. Codd, E.F.: A relational model of data for large shared data banks. Commun. ACM **13**(6), 377–387 (1970). https://doi.org/10.1145/362384.362685
9. Configit: B2B Manufacturing Insights Q3 2023 (2023). https://content.configit.com/story/q3-2023-quarterly-newsletter
10. Friedenthal, S., Moore, A., Steiner, R.: A Practical Guide to SysML: The Systems Modeling Language. Morgan Kaufmann (2014)
11. Haav, H., Maigre, R.: A semantic model for product configuration in timber industry. In: A. Lupeikiene, O. Vasilecas, G. Dzemyda (eds.) Databases and Information Systems X - Selected Papers from the Thirteenth International Baltic Conference, DB&IS 2018, Trakai, Lithuania, July 1–4, 2018, Frontiers in Artificial Intelligence and Applications, vol. 315, pp. 143–158. IOS Press (2018). https://doi.org/10.3233/978-1-61499-941-6-143
12. Kang, K.C., Cohen, S.G., Hess, J.A., Novak, W.E., Peterson, A.S.: Feature-oriented domain analysis (FODA) feasibility study. Software Engineering Institute, Carnegie Mellon University. Technical Report (1990)
13. Katuu, S.: Enterprise resource planning: past, present, and future. New Rev. Inf. Netw. **25**(1), 37–46 (2020)
14. Kumar, V., Reinartz, W.: Customer Relationship Management. Springer (2018)
15. Object Management Group: Object Constraint Language 2.3.1 (2011). https://www.omg.org/spec/OCL/2.3.1
16. Salesforce: What is Salesforce CPQ? (2024). https://www.salesforce.com/eu/sales/cpq/what-is-salesforce-cpq/
17. Smirnov, A.V., Shilov, N., Kashevnik, A.M., Jung, T., Sinko, M., Oroszi, A.: Ontology-driven product configuration - industrial use case. In: Filipe, J., Liu, K. (eds.) KMIS 2011 - Proceedings of the International Conference on Knowledge Management and Information Sharing, Paris, France, 26–29 October, 2011, pp. 38–47. SciTePress (2011)
18. Soininen, T., Tiihonen, J., Männistö, T., Sulonen, R.: Towards a general ontology of configuration. Artif. Intell. Eng. Des. Anal. Manuf. **12**(4), 357–372 (1998). http://journals.cambridge.org/action/displayAbstract?aid=38651
19. Stadtler, H.: Supply chain management: An overview. In: H. Stadtler, C. Kilger, H. Meyr (eds.) Supply Chain Management and Advanced Planning: Concepts, Models, Software, and Case Studies, pp. 3–28. Springer, Berlin Heidelberg, Berlin, Heidelberg (2015). https://doi.org/10.1007/978-3-642-55309-7_1
20. Stark, J.: Product lifecycle management (plm). In: Product Lifecycle Management (Volume 1): 21st Century Paradigm for Product Realisation, pp. 1–32. Springer International Publishing, Cham (2022). https://doi.org/10.1007/978-3-030-98578-3_1
21. Warmer, J., Kleppe, A.: The Object Constraint Language: Precise Modeling with UML. Addison-Wesley (1998)
22. Wertel, S.: Parameter models: How CLM ties it all together (2020). https://configit.com/learn/blog/parameter-models-how-clm-ties-it-all-together/
23. Yang, D., Miao, R., Wu, H., Zhou, Y.: Product configuration knowledge modeling using ontology web language. Expert Syst. Appl. **36**(3), 4399–4411 (2009). https://doi.org/10.1016/J.ESWA.2008.05.026
24. Zeeb, M.: From idea to operations - how Configit and adesso are closing the gap between product configuration and order fulfilment (2025). https://www.adesso.de/en/news/blog/from-idea-to-operations-how-configit-and-adesso-are-closing-the-gap-between-product-configuration-and-order-fulfilment.jsp

**Open Access** This chapter is licensed under the terms of the Creative Commons Attribution-NonCommercial-NoDerivatives 4.0 International License (http://creativecommons.org/licenses/by-nc-nd/4.0/), which permits any noncommercial use, sharing, distribution and reproduction in any medium or format, as long as you give appropriate credit to the original author(s) and the source, provide a link to the Creative Commons license and indicate if you modified the licensed material. You do not have permission under this license to share adapted material derived from this chapter or parts of it.

The images or other third party material in this chapter are included in the chapter's Creative Commons license, unless indicated otherwise in a credit line to the material. If material is not included in the chapter's Creative Commons license and your intended use is not permitted by statutory regulation or exceeds the permitted use, you will need to obtain permission directly from the copyright holder.

# Chapter 4
# Modeling

**Abstract** Product modeling is the specification of the product variety and also comprises the necessary reasoning, the user interface, interfaces to other business processes, IT, etc. It relies on a set of generic concepts like part trees, type hierarchy, feature values, table constraints, etc., to distinguish the instance (application) and model (domain) layers.
This chapter focuses on theoretical and practical aspects of representing product configuration problems effectively. It introduces three layers of representation in product configuration, provides details on several aspects important in modeling configurable products, and introduces an UML-based modeling notation.

Model-based engineering [2, 24, 29] organizes the world and the knowledge about it into three layers: the physical world (L0), models of the world (L1), and meta-models (L2) which describe models and models of models, and models of models of models, etc.

Seeing product configuration in that way, we can distinguish the following layers of representations and avoid misunderstandings by clearly stating what we are talking about:

- L0: Configuration instances, i.e., the individually configured product (e.g., my mountain bike is red).
- L1: Configuration model, i.e., the specification of the configurable product family (e.g., Bicycle has a feature Color and a Frame as a part).
- L2: Configuration concepts, i.e., the expressiveness of the modeling tools (e.g., type, feature, sub-part).

Software product line engineering (feature modeling [12]) takes a similar approach by distinguishing domain engineering (modeling on L1) and application engineering (configuration on L0). In addition, it adds a second dimension by separating the problem space (what are the requirements) from the solution space (how they are resolved). Figure 4.1 shows that using a configurator (i.e., the box on the lower right) requires both proper domain knowledge implemented into logic by the knowledge engineer (i.e., the upper right box) and a clear specification of the requirements by the customer based on the provided user interface (i.e., the lower left box).

© Siemens Aktiengesellschaft Österreich 2026

R. Comploi-Taupe and A. Falkner, *Product Configuration*,
SpringerBriefs in Computer Science,
https://doi.org/10.1007/978-3-032-17163-4_4

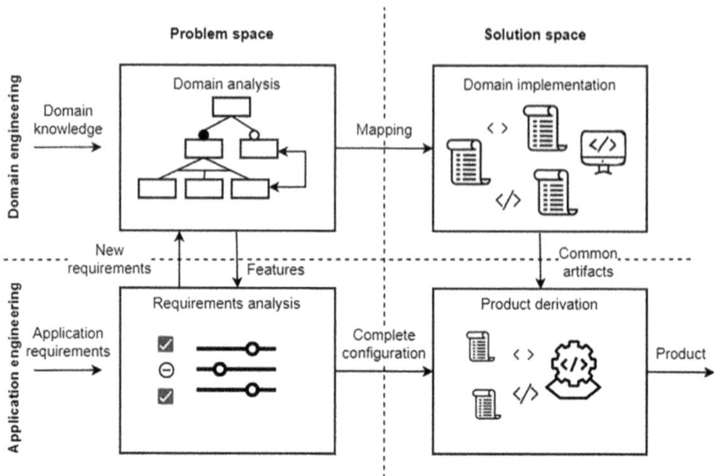


**Fig. 4.1** Distinguishing the layers in product modeling (*Source* [12])

The core of all this is understanding the product and formalizing the product knowledge in the problem space (i.e., the upper left box): Product managers and knowledge engineers define the product structure and variety, including the decision options (i.e., features) for customers, e.g., as a feature model which is easily understandable to domain experts as well. Once they have a clear understanding what customers want, knowledge engineers, together with IT experts, map this to a solution with a user interface, logic, data import and export, and document generation. They either choose a knowledge base in the representation for the tools of a reputable configurator vendor or a proprietary implementation. On the other hand, customers use exactly the same model (and a hopefully effective user interface) to select the features they need to achieve an optimally fitting product.

The two layers, modeling (variability management) and individual configuration, comprise many aspects, as summarized in Fig. 4.2. On the instance level, customers use a user interface to create their configurations (i.e., the customized products) and to extract the necessary output, which typically consists of quotes, a Bill of Materials, and a Bill of Processes for manufacturing.

In order to get valid and good solutions, users need the help of a solver to do the reasoning based on the knowledge base. In addition, they will typically need some sort of persistency (i.e., a database) and the usual IT landscape (servers, policies, etc.). To make this available at the instance level for their customers, vendors need to model the variety of their offering. That means the product structure and the constraints. This builds upon product information that typically comes from a product data management system and requires a good modeling tool to create consistent and maintainable models.

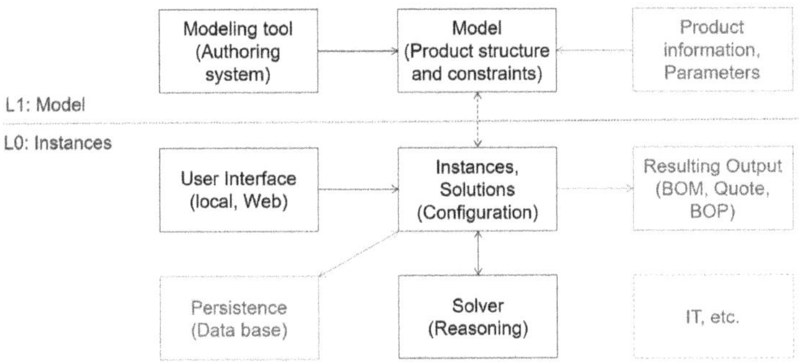


**Fig. 4.2** Modeling the product configuration scope (*Source* Own work)

## 4.1 Modeling Aspects

We will now go into more detail, focusing on important challenges in the aspects of modeling, reasoning, user and data interfaces, versioning, and IT in general. This is a comprehensive overview of the necessary content of any configuration system and can be seen as an explanation of layer L2 from above, whereas Sect. 4.2 presents a specific example of such a meta-model (an UML-like notation for product specification).

### *Modeling (The Variety)*

There is a lot to be specified, starting from the variability, the part-of structure, the kind-of hierarchy (i.e., specialization of all the properties and even the structure) [1, 4, 26, 27, 33]. There might be relations between the components, not only tree-like, but arbitrary graphs, or even resources or functions. And of course, there are many different types and representations of constraints.

A huge topic is finding the right prices based on costs and competition. Because all parts are normally connected with some costs, vendors want to optimize their margin. This might be very country-specific and dependent on the customer situation (and is therefore connected to CRM, cf. Chap. 3).

The following aspects are relevant in modeling:

- Variability (also called variety, specialization, classification): The product and its parts come in different kinds (e.g., forms or materials) which can lead to a potentially deep hierarchy of sub-types.

- Properties (also called attributes, features, or characteristics): They have various types, domains, and units (e.g., centimeter, inch, or currencies).
- Structure: Typically, this forms a tree of sub-parts (components) with a defined or (partially) open number of parts (multiplicity, cardinality).
- Relations: In addition to this rather restricted tree, arbitrary relations (cross-tree connections) lead to a network (graph) of dependencies [6].
- Resources: Often, some properties represent quantities that are produced and consumed by different parts of the product, e.g., electric power. They may be coded in a special way to ensure balance or sufficient supply [27].
- Functions: These are also special properties that can be a bit tricky because they often relate to the product but are realized by a subset of its parts, e.g., user requirements concerning the functionality or performance of the product. Realization variants (even different structures) must be mapped to function values.
- Constraints: In real products, there are many restrictions on structure, property values and relations. Some of them are hard (i.e., must be obeyed at all times), others are soft (e.g., user preferences, effects on costs, etc.) [20].
- Pricing: This is a huge field and sometimes seen separate from pure configuration.[1] It comprises sales strategy, margins, approvals, country-specific aspects, and much more. However, it makes sense to integrate it with configuration because of the dependence of prices on user decisions.

## *Reasoning (Solving)*

There are different reasoning tasks [7, 8, 10, 20]. Finding a solution is also called solving. Often, it is not sufficient to find only one solution, e.g., because the first solution is not good enough. Then it helps to list all solutions (in a certain context) to allow a user to choose from among all correct and feasible products. If this is too cumbersome for the user, they may want to let the system auto-complete the configuration task based on the decisions already made. Here, the system should find the best solution with respect to some minimality or maximality condition; that is, it needs to solve an optimization problem.[2]

Some systems allow inconsistent or partial configurations that do not lead to a valid solution. Then users want assistance to repair them in some way; that is, to retract some decisions so that a valid solution can be achieved.

---

[1] That is mirrored in the term CPQ (Configure—Price—Quote) where Pricing is at the same level as Configuration. By the way, we cover Quoting in the subsection "Interfaces to other systems" below because it typically involves dedicated tools.

[2] For example, a user might desire to find a configured product with the lowest $CO_2$ footprint, see Chap. 9.

The following are typically relevant reasoning tasks:

- Check the correctness of the configuration.
- Find a solution.
- Find all solutions.
- Complete a current partial configuration to a valid solution.
- Repair a current inconsistent configuration to a valid solution.
- Find the best (i.e., minimal or maximal) solution (optimization).


## *User Interface*

The user interface is another very important part of a configurator. It needs to align precisely with the logic, but also make it easy for the user to configure and understand the product. Thus, workflows or user groups may help, as can various types of assistants (e.g., recommendations).

The sales department must decide upon the channels and accessibility: on-site installation, cloud or web application, for PCs only or also for mobile devices, for online use only or also offline.


The following aspects should be considered w.r.t. UIs:

- User groups: Who will use the configuration system? End-customers? Sales? Pre-sales? Resellers? Business partners? Order validation? Service?
- Workflows: Each user group has different ways of working efficiently (e.g., end-customers may take just a few decisions and let auto-completion do the rest, whereas order validation wants to look at details and quickly jump to specific positions in the whole product tree).
- Components and groups: Users can benefit from groupings of the product in the UI that are independent of the configuration logic (and instead target specific user groups, for example).
- Decentralized and collaborative modeling: Country-specific knowledge about products may be maintained decentrally, and multiple users might work on the same product model or configuration simultaneously.
- Web application: The look-and-feel needs to comply with standards that the user knows and the different browsers support. On the other hand, it must also comply with the company's guidelines and offer a unique and good user experience.
- Mobile devices: The user interface must adapt to smaller screens and limited communication bandwidth.
- Offline usage: In some cases, the configurator must also work without an internet connection (e.g., in some rural areas or in shielded buildings such as basements).

- Assistance: Visualizations (e.g., what-you-see-is-what-you-get), explanations (e.g., why certain selections are no longer allowed), recommendations (e.g., better alternatives, auto-completion, added value), and chatbots (see Chap. 8).

## Interfaces to Other Systems

In order to use the configuration results in the product lifecycle, we need many interfaces to other systems like customer relationship management, product data management, supply chain management, or interfaces to CAD (computer-aided design) systems. And the results must be represented in various formats; for example, to generate quotes for customers and technical drawings for production, as well as price lists and manuals.

The following aspects are relevant in the area of interfaces:

- Presentation of results: quotes, technical plans, etc.
- Interface to CRM (Customer Relationship Management), e.g., Salesforce, for pricing and quoting.
- Alignment with PDM (Product Data Management) and SCM (Supply Chain Management), e.g., Teamcenter, SAP [5].
- Interface to CAD: 2D or 3D, view-only (e.g., showing a fully rendered image of the result that can be zoomed and inspected) or allowing even changes (i.e., a fully integrated visual editor).

## Versioning

Versioning is a very important aspect of the configuration of long-lived systems. The installed base (either in a persistent database or some file storage) contains the information about a configured system which was installed somewhere. Inevitably, a need for change will arise (either due to extension or to repair). But in the interim, the product model will have changed, and the system in the installed base (which was configured based on an old model) may no longer comply with the new model. How to deal with such a situation under the pressure to avoid unnecessary costs? There are concepts such as reconfiguration, knowledge evolution, and regression testing.

The following aspects need to be considered:

- Persistence: Data can be stored in a database (e.g., SQL), a knowledge graph [4], or some proprietary file formats.

- Reconfiguration: This means that a finished configuration result is changed at some later time (e.g., between the initial offer and the final customer order, or for an extension after deployment) [22, 30].
- Knowledge Evolution: Reconfiguration—but also maintenance of an installed product—will sooner or later require adjusting the existing configuration to the latest model. To reduce efforts, this must be highly automated. Perhaps some remaining inconsistencies or ambiguities need to be resolved manually by an expert [16].
- Testing is vital to ensure quality (see Chap. 6). Test cases and scripts must be continuously adapted to changes in the model and executed for each release (regression testing) [11, 18].
- Debugging is necessary when tests fail. Modeling tools must provide functionality to efficiently find modeling errors, e.g., based on diagnosis technology [14, 15].
- Deployment must be fully automated and ensure quality by running the regression tests, so that stable daily releases are possible.

## *IT Topics*

All the aspects above depend heavily on the existing (or planned) IT landscape in the company. Typically, there are internal regulations and/or conventions concerning access, hardware resources, software licenses, training and user support, etc. We touched upon some of these issues in Chap. 3 but will not cover the major part in this book, because the challenges are not specific to configuration and there is much literature available concerning DevOps solutions in general.

Just to mention some aspects to consider:

- Authentication/authorization
- Security
- Integration into the existing IT landscape
- Hardware/software stack
- Performance and scalability
- Support/training.

## 4.2  Modeling Notation

Many representations for configuration knowledge have been proposed over several decades: apart from domain-specific languages, trees and tables are the easiest ones to use and understand by modelers and domain experts. Examples are Product

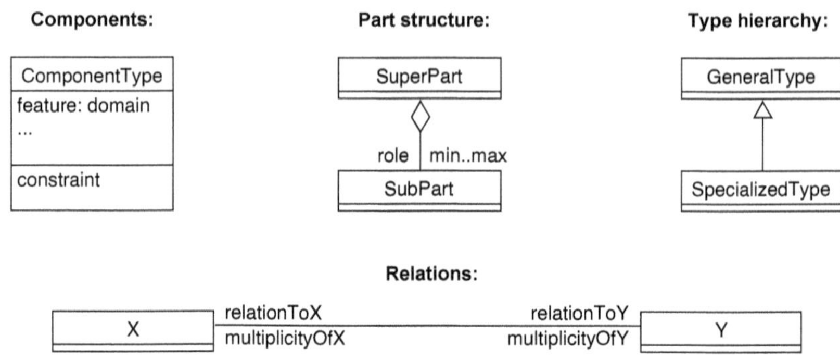

**Fig. 4.3**  A comprehensive modeling notation based on UML class diagrams (*Source* Own work)


Variant Master [19], Feature Models [21],[3] and Variant Tables [17].[4] We prefer an approach based on UML class diagrams [9, 13, 15, 25, 28] because they are more powerful:[5] They can represent arbitrary part-of and kind-of hierarchies and can easily be extended with constraints (as tables and even formulas in a language called Object Constraint Language (OCL) [23, 32]). This also goes beyond the proprietary representations of many configurator vendors, which typically use a structure with expandable folders (similar to a file explorer) and windows for editing collections of properties. UML class diagrams can also be easily represented in various textual languages; see Chap. 8 for a JSON-based representation language for product configuration, and OOASP [10] (cf. Sect. 5.4) for a representation language based on UML class diagrams and logic programming.[6]

Figure 4.3 shows the main building blocks of our comprehensive notation:

- Components (more precisely: component types) with properties (features with various domains such as Boolean, enumerations, integer ranges, etc.) and constraints (formulas). For these, we use UML classes, attributes, and methods.
- Part structure: each part relation can be named individually (needed when the same component type can be used in multiple part roles, e.g., front wheel and back wheel of a bicycle), and its cardinality (multiplicity of subparts) can be restricted

---

[3] See Sect. 5.2 for more on Feature Models.

[4] See Sect. 5.1 for more on Variant Tables.

[5] Even more powerful than the extended FM notation of Cardinality-Based Feature Models [3].

[6] In this way, our restricted UML diagrams get a formal semantics as they can be automatically translated into concise representations—either directly into some logics, as was done by Felfernig et al. [13], or via an unambiguous intermediate representation like an ontology [4]. For the transformation of a specific product model, potential target languages could be filtered out if they do not support all used concepts.

(by default, it allows zero to many subparts). For this, we use UML aggregations[7] with the implicit cardinality of exactly 1 for the super-part.

- Type hierarchy: for the specialization of concepts, such as machine—vehicle—motor vehicle—bus—school bus. For this, we use UML inheritance (complete and disjoint[8]).
- Arbitrary relations between components, each side with a mandatory role name and an optional cardinality (similar to part relations). For them, we use general UML associations.[9]
- The format of constraint tables is straightforward; an example is shown in Fig. 4.4.

## Example

Models for our running example about folding bikes have already been shown: Figs. 2.4 and 2.5 in Chap. 2 show two different instances of the configurable folding bike, i.e., L0 representations. Figure 2.3 shows an L1 configuration model for this configurable product. An extended version of this configuration model can be found in Fig. 3.5. The L2 model used for these models is the meta-model of UML class diagrams.

Let us illustrate the modeling concepts with another example that is based on a real-world configuration problem [7, 10]. In Fig. 4.4, we model the hardware racks example from Fig. 2.1 in Chap. 2 with our UML notation and constraint tables. It is just one of many ways to model that product—depending on conventions and the advantages/disadvantages of individual design decisions.

- The part tree (on the left-hand side of the diagram) has depth 3: HwRack is the root and consists of an upper Frame, an optional lower Frame, and a Powersupply. A Frame consists of one or two Rows (in different positions).
- Modules are not subparts but are assigned to a Row via a relation. There is a subtle difference between subpart relations and arbitrary relations concerning creation and deletion of object instances during reasoning: subparts are created and deleted together with their superpart, whereas for arbitrary relations, no instances are created (nor deleted); however, available (free) instances may be used. Furthermore, relations can have cardinalities greater than 1 on both sides (whereas a superpart always has cardinality 1).

---

[7] We prefer aggregations (hollow diamond) over compositions (filled diamond) because they convey the meaning that subparts can exist independently from the super-part, which is typical for assembled products where parts exist on their own (e.g., in a supply store) but have a super-part when mounted.

[8] We do not allow multiple inheritance. We recommend not to instantiate classes that have subclasses.

[9] Non-part relations occur often in real-world products, e.g., for neighbor relationships, peer-to-peer connections, or other graph-like structures. We decided to model them independently from part relations which form the main tree structure of the product and are used for many practical tasks such as the UI or BOM.

- The type hierarchy has depth 3 as well: a Module can be either narrow or wide, and both subtypes can be specialized further (e.g., a ModuleNarrow is either a CPU or a ModuleNarrow4). All other components come in two variants (subtypes), except for the HwRack itself.[10]

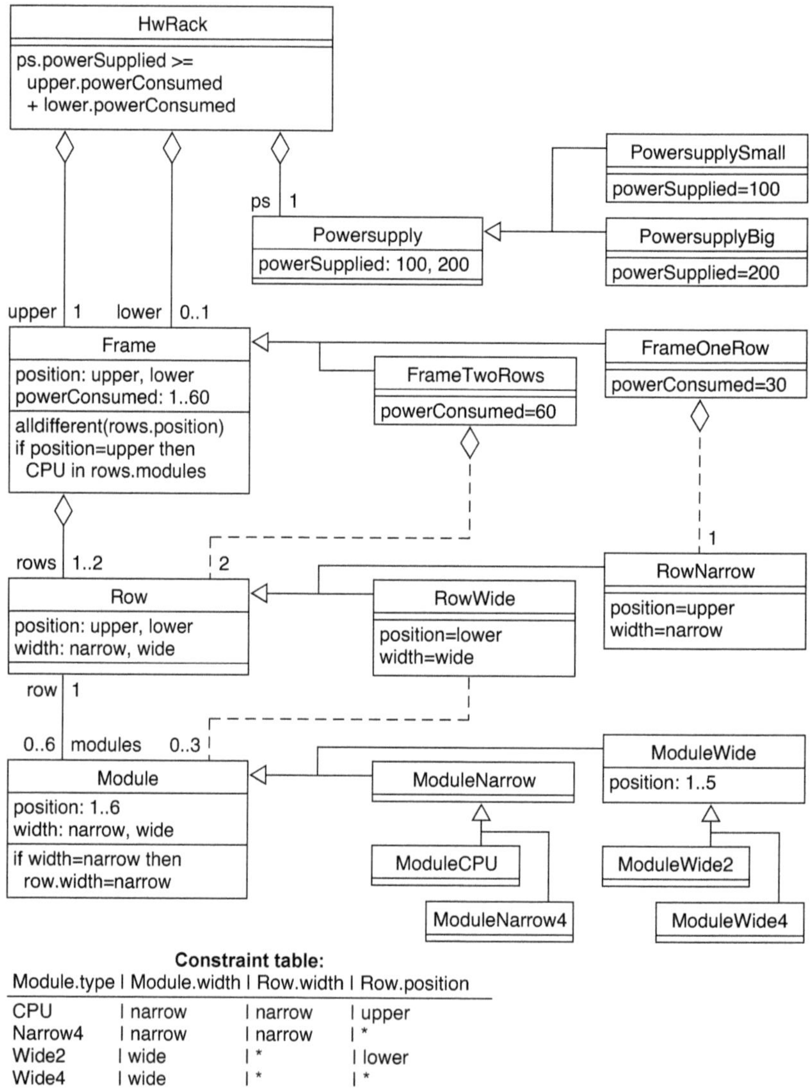

**Fig. 4.4** Modeling example with UML class diagrams and tables: Hardware racks (*Source* Own work)

---

[10] If we always needed a facing component where there is no frame, then the lower frame would not be optional, and we would need a pseudo frame as a third type.

- The subtypes (i.e., specialized types) set values for some of the features of the (abstract) general types; e.g., a small power supply supplies only 100 W power, whereas a big power supply supplies 200. This can be expressed as a simple formula in the constraint section of the component definition or, more naturally, in a constraint table; e.g., Module.width in the example at the bottom of the diagram.
- But they can also specialize the feature domain; e.g., the position of a wide module cannot be the last (narrow) slot; therefore, the range is restricted to 1..5 (instead of 1..6).
- Even the cardinalities of subparts and arbitrary relations can be specialized; e.g., FrameOneRow has only one RowNarrow as a subpart, whereas FrameTwoRow always has two Rows. And a row for wide modules can house maximally three modules, not 6, as the other row type(s).[11]
- Constraint tables are an easy way to specify allowed combinations of feature values; e.g., narrow modules must be placed in RowNarrow, whereas wide modules can go in any Row (expressed by the asterisk wildcard in the table). ModuleCPU is only allowed in upper rows; ModuleWide2 is only allowed in lower rows.
- More complicated constraints are expressed as formulas; e.g., the resource constraint in HwRack (which ensures the total consumed power is less than or equal to the supplied power[12]) or the constraint for the mandatory CPU in upper Frames.

## Exercises

**Exercise 4.1** Revisit the folding bike constraints from the CRM/Sales view in the Example in Chap. 3 and present them as a constraint table.

**Exercise 4.2** Present more folding bike constraints, such as those from Sects. 3.2 to 3.4, as constraint tables.

**Exercise 4.3** Does the model (Fig. 4.4) of the hardware rack example in Sect. 4.2 fully represent the customer's intention? Are apparently incorrect configurations possible? If so, how can they be prohibited? *Hint:* Check the potential module positions.

**Exercise 4.4** Sketch a good user interface for the hardware rack example in Sect. 4.2. What are your envisioned user groups and workflows?

**Exercise 4.5** The product manager for hardware racks in the example in Sect. 4.2 decides that wide modules in upper rows are only allowed at positions 1, 3, and 5. What changes to the model (Fig. 4.4) are necessary? How can knowledge evolution be implemented? Can all already configured hardware racks be automatically evolved?

---

[11] For space reasons, the role names were not written for the specialized relations, and association specialization [31] is not visually shown.

[12] In reality, the calculation of consumed power is based on the actually placed modules in the rows of the frames of the rack.

**Exercise 4.6** Create a configuration model according to Sect. 4.2 for the following product:

- A bicycle offering depends on user requirements.
- They may be used at night and/or for sport (which can be restricted to road or off-road).
- Bicycles have a type (city, mountain, racing) and optionally an e-motor and/or a light.
- There are some manufacturing restrictions: City bikes always have a light; mountain bikes can have a light and must have one if they also have an e-motor; racing bikes have neither a light nor an e-motor.
- Night use requires a light.
- Sport use disallows city bikes.
- Road use requires a racing bike.
- Off-road use requires a mountain bike.
- Sport use disallows an e-motor.

List all feasible variants of the offering. Can all combinations of user requirements be covered?

# References


1. Abbasi, E.K., Leclercq, T., Heymans, P.: A meta-model for product configuration ontologies. In: Felfernig, A., Fuentes, L., Cleland-Huang, J., Assunção, W.K.G., Quinton, C., Guo, J., Schmid, K., Huchard, M., Ayala, I., Rojas, J.M., Le, V., Horcas, J.M. (eds.) SPLC '22: 26th ACM International Systems and Software Product Line Conference, Graz, Austria, September 12–16, 2022, Volume B, pp. 166–173. ACM (2022). https://doi.org/10.1145/3503229.3547044
2. Atkinson, C., Kuhne, T.: Model-driven development: a metamodeling foundation. IEEE Softw. **20**(5), 36–41 (2003). https://doi.org/10.1109/MS.2003.1231149
3. Bak, K., Diskin, Z., Antkiewicz, M., Czarnecki, K., Wasowski, A.: Clafer: unifying class and feature modeling. Softw. Syst. Model. **15**(3), 811–845 (2016). https://doi.org/10.1007/S10270-014-0441-1
4. Bischof, S., Falkner, A., Schneider, P., Steyskal, S., Topa, M.: CONTO: An ontology-based approach for interoperable configuration knowledge. In: SEMANTiCS'25: International Conference on Semantic Systems (2025)
5. Blumöhr, U., Münch, M., Ukalovic, M.: Variant Configuration with SAP, 2nd edn. SAP PRESS (2011)
6. Dhungana, D., Falkner, A.A., Haselböck, A.: Generation of conjoint domain models for system-of-systems. In: Järvi, J., Kästner, C. (eds.) Generative Programming: Concepts and Experiences, GPCE'13, Indianapolis, IN, USA - October 27–28, 2013, pp. 159–168. ACM (2013). https://doi.org/10.1145/2517208.2517224
7. Falkner, A.A., Friedrich, G., Haselböck, A., Schenner, G., Schreiner, H.: Twenty-five years of successful application of constraint technologies at Siemens. AI Mag. **37**(4), 67–80 (2016). https://doi.org/10.1609/AIMAG.V37I4.2688
8. Falkner, A.A., Haselböck, A., Krames, G., Schenner, G., Schreiner, H., Taupe, R.: Solver requirements for interactive configuration. J. Univers. Comput. Sci. **26**(3), 343–373 (2020). http://www.jucs.org/jucs_26_3/solver_requirements_for_interactive

9. Falkner, A.A., Haselböck, A., Schenner, G., Schreiner, H.: Modeling and solving technical product configuration problems. Artif. Intell. Eng. Des. Anal. Manuf. **25**(2), 115–129 (2011). https://doi.org/10.1017/S089006041000570

10. Falkner, A.A., Ryabokon, A., Schenner, G., Shchekotykhin, K.M.: OOASP: connecting object-oriented and logic programming. In: Calimeri, F., Ianni, G., Truszczynski, M. (eds.) Logic Programming and Nonmonotonic Reasoning - 13th International Conference, LPNMR 2015, Lexington, KY, USA, September 27–30, 2015. Proceedings, Lecture Notes in Computer Science, vol. 9345, pp. 332–345. Springer (2015). https://doi.org/10.1007/978-3-319-23264-5_28

11. Falkner, A.A., Schenner, G., Friedrich, G., Ryabokon, A.: Testing object-oriented configurators with ASP. In: Mayer, W., Albert, P. (eds.) Proceedings of the Workshop on Configuration at ECAI 2012, Montpellier, France, August 27, 2012, CEUR Workshop Proceedings, vol. 958, pp. 21–26. CEUR-WS.org (2012). https://ceur-ws.org/Vol-958/paper4.pdf

12. Felfernig, A., Falkner, A., Benavides, D.: Feature Models: AI-Driven Design, Analysis and Applications. SpringerBriefs in Computer Science. Springer International Publishing, Cham (2024). https://doi.org/10.1007/978-3-031-61874-1

13. Felfernig, A., Friedrich, G., Jannach, D.: UML as domain specific language for the construction of knowledge-based configuration systems. Int. J. Software Eng. Knowl. Eng. **10**(04), 449–469 (2000). https://doi.org/10.1142/s0218194000000249

14. Felfernig, A., Friedrich, G., Jannach, D., Stumptner, M.: Consistency-based diagnosis of configuration knowledge bases. Artif. Intell. **152**(2), 213–234 (2004)

15. Friedrich, G., Jannach, D., Stumptner, M., Zanker, M.: Knowledge engineering for configuration systems. In: A. Felfernig, L. Hotz, C. Bagley, J. Tiihonen (eds.) Knowledge-based Configuration: From Research to Business Cases, 1st edn., chap. 11, pp. 139–155. Morgan Kaufmann Publishers Inc., San Francisco, CA, USA (2014)

16. Friedrich, G., Ryabokon, A., Falkner, A.A., Haselböck, A., Schenner, G., Schreiner, H.: (re)configuration based on model generation. In: Drescher, C., Lynce, I., Treinen, R. (eds.) Proceedings Second Workshop on Logics for Component Configuration, LoCoCo 2011, Perugia, Italy, 12th September 2011, EPTCS, vol. 65, pp. 26–35 (2011). https://doi.org/10.4204/EPTCS.65.3

17. Haag, A., Haag, L.: Further empowering variant tables for mass customization. Int. J. Ind. Eng. Manag. **10**(2), 155–170 (2019). https://doi.org/10.24867/IJIEM-2019-2-236

18. Herud, K., Baumeister, J.: Testing product configuration knowledge bases declaratively. In: Reuss, P., Eisenstadt, V., Schönborn, J.M., Schäfer, J. (eds.) Proceedings of the LWDA 2022 Workshops: FGWM, FGKD, and FGDB, Hildesheim (Germany), Oktober 5–7th, 2022, CEUR Workshop Proceedings, vol. 3341, pp. 173–186. CEUR-WS.org (2022). https://ceur-ws.org/Vol-3341/WM-LWDA_2022_CRC_4316.pdf

19. Hvam, L., Mortensen, N.H., Riis, J.: Product Customization. Springer (2008)

20. Junker, U.: Configuration. In: Rossi, F., van Beek, P., Walsh, T. (eds.) Handbook of Constraint Programming, pp. 837–873. Elsevier Science (2006)

21. Kang, K.C., Cohen, S.G., Hess, J.A., Novak, W.E., Peterson, A.S.: Feature-oriented domain analysis (FODA) feasibility study. Software Engineering Institute, Carnegie Mellon University, Technical Report (1990)

22. Manhart, P.: Reconfiguration – a problem in search of solutions. In: Jannach, D., Felfernig, A. (eds.) Papers from the Configuration Workshop at IJCAI'05, pp. 64–67 (2005)

23. Object Management Group: Object Constraint Language 2.3.1 (2011). https://www.omg.org/spec/OCL/2.3.1

24. Object Management Group: Meta object facility (2016). https://www.omg.org/spec/MOF

25. Object Management Group: Unified Modeling Language 2.5.1, section 11.4, Classes (2017). https://www.omg.org/spec/UML/2.5.1

26. Sabin, D., Weigel, R.: Product configuration frameworks - a survey. IEEE Intell. Syst. **13**(4), 42–49 (1998). https://doi.org/10.1109/5254.708432

27. Soininen, T., Tiihonen, J., Männistö, T., Sulonen, R.: Towards a general ontology of configuration. Artif. Intell. Eng. Des. Anal. Manuf. **12**(4), 357–372 (1998). https://doi.org/10.1017/S0890060498124083

28. Sommerville, I.: Software Engineering, 10th edn. Pearson Higher Ed (2016)
29. Strahringer, S.: Ein sprachbasierter Metamodellbegriff und seine Verallgemeinerung durch das Konzept des Metaisierungsprinzips. In: Pohl, K., Schürr, A., Vossen, G. (eds.) Modellierung '98, Proceedings des GI-Workshops in Münster, 11.-13. März 1998, CEUR Workshop Proceedings, vol. 9. CEUR-WS.org (1998). https://ceur-ws.org/Vol-9/Strahringer.ps
30. Stumptner, M., Wotawa, F.: Model-based reconfiguration. In: Artificial Intelligence in Design'98, pp. 45–64. Springer (1998)
31. Taupe, R., Falkner, A., Schenner, G.: Deriving tighter component cardinality bounds for product configuration. In: 18th International Configuration Workshop, pp. 47–54 (2016). http://cp2016.a4cp.org/program/workshops/CWS-2016-Proceedings.pdf
32. Warmer, J., Kleppe, A.: The object constraint language: precise modeling with UML. Addison-Wesley (1998)
33. Yang, D., Miao, R., Wu, H., Zhou, Y.: Product configuration knowledge modeling using ontology web language. Expert Syst. Appl. **36**(3), 4399–4411 (2009). https://doi.org/10.1016/J.ESWA.2008.05.026

**Open Access** This chapter is licensed under the terms of the Creative Commons Attribution-NonCommercial-NoDerivatives 4.0 International License (http://creativecommons.org/licenses/by-nc-nd/4.0/), which permits any noncommercial use, sharing, distribution and reproduction in any medium or format, as long as you give appropriate credit to the original author(s) and the source, provide a link to the Creative Commons license and indicate if you modified the licensed material. You do not have permission under this license to share adapted material derived from this chapter or parts of it.

The images or other third party material in this chapter are included in the chapter's Creative Commons license, unless indicated otherwise in a credit line to the material. If material is not included in the chapter's Creative Commons license and your intended use is not permitted by statutory regulation or exceeds the permitted use, you will need to obtain permission directly from the copyright holder.

# Chapter 5
# Configuration Technologies

**Abstract** Technologies for solving configuration problems must deal with complex problems and huge solution spaces. Knowledge-based reasoning is a family of approaches that separate declarative problem specifications from problem-independent solving mechanisms. In this chapter, we present overviews of important knowledge-based approaches suited for configuration: variant tables, feature models, rule-based systems, logics, and constraint programming. Finally, we briefly describe commercial configuration solutions.

Before we explore existing technologies and tools for product configuration, let us look at the challenges, based on an example: Interlocking systems ensure safe railway traffic operations and comprise a lot of customized hardware[1] and software, needed to monitor and control the sensors and actuators on the railway tracks, such as signals, switches, or vacancy detectors (cf. Figs. 5.1 and 5.2).

In the early 1990s, co-author Andreas Falkner joined Siemens to develop a configurator for railway interlocking systems [21]. The configurator has been in operation for more than 30 years and is still being further developed due to new types of safety equipment and changed regulations. Meanwhile, it consists of 1.5 million lines of code, thousands of classes, and hundreds of projects (i.e., completed configurations of different railway stations in different countries). The typical size of a problem is 2,000,000 variables (i.e., decisions about properties or relations) and 1,000,000 constraints.

Let us do some calculations to get a feeling for the complexity of product configuration. Consider just a very small railway station consisting of two switches and four signals, where each can occur in one of 10 variants (these components are highlighted by red boxes in Fig. 5.3).

The number of variants of a complete station can be easily calculated by simple multiplication:[2] Two switches with 10 variants means $10 \times 10 = 100$ variants for the two switches in total. Four signals with 10 variants means $10^4 = 10,000$ variants for the signals. And for the total number we multiply again and get $100 \times 10,000 = 1,000,000$ variants.

---

[1] Such as described in Figs. 2.1 and 4.4.

[2] See Chap. 7 for more details on such calculations.

© Siemens Aktiengesellschaft Österreich 2026
R. Comploi-Taupe and A. Falkner, *Product Configuration*,
SpringerBriefs in Computer Science,
https://doi.org/10.1007/978-3-032-17163-4_5

**Fig. 5.1** A workplace in a railway control center (*Source* Siemens [21])

**Fig. 5.2** Railway interlocking system hardware (*Source* Siemens [21])

**Fig. 5.3** A tiny railway station with two switches and four signals (photo taken by Andreas Falkner)

In reality, the solution space is confined by some constraints [68]. For example, imagine that there is a constraint that all signals must occur in the same variant. Since the variety of the switches stays the same independently of this constraint (still 100 variants), and only the first signal can be freely selected from one of its 10 possible variants (whereas the variant of all remaining signals is uniquely determined by that), the total number of valid variants of the station (i.e., complying with the constraint) is just $100 \times 10 = 1000$, which is much less than the number of variants without the constraint.

In reality, these numbers are much higher, since real-world railway stations are much more complex. We have not only two but many more types of elements, and many more parameters. For a tiny realistic station with two tracks, we already reach $10^{90}$ possible solutions, which is far beyond the number of atoms in the universe. But roughly only one billion of those are technically and economically feasible. The challenge of finding one of these feasible solutions is thus like the proverbial search for a needle in a haystack.

And we run into the problem of exponential growth: For large real-world stations, we have millions of parameters. The exponential growth connected to the multiplication of those parameters is a huge challenge. Just adding one parameter with two values typically doubles the size of the problem. In the worst case, this also means doubled memory consumption. So, if the problem increases only a little bit, we might run out of memory very fast.

Most approaches to handle this challenge are based on knowledge-based reasoning, sometimes also called model-based reasoning [62]. It goes back to Bob Kowalski's famous equation: Algorithm = Logic + Control [45]. The logic part is there to describe exactly what the problem is, whereas the control part deals with the procedural aspects: how to solve the problem, how to find a solution.

This is in contrast to the traditional way of implementing solving algorithms via imperative (procedural) programming, where the representation of the problem is a coded program that also includes the knowledge *how* to solve the problem. Imperative programming bears some disadvantages because the "what" and the "how" are intermingled in the program, which tends to make maintenance more difficult [21].

Model-based or declarative approaches typically perform better for product configuration problems by separating responsibilities.[3] A domain expert states the problem, and a knowledge engineer formalizes that knowledge into a declarative model which is a clear specification of what is needed to be achieved. Generic solvers can work with such declarative models as input and deliver results. These generic solvers are typically supplied by some tool providers who put a lot of effort into the performance of the solvers and test them on applications from diverse domains [57]. Therefore, generic solvers together with adequate declarative problem specifications often perform better than ad hoc imperative implementations. And declarative approaches typically offer additional benefits such as conciseness and maintainability of the problem specifications [21, 43].

---

[3] See Fig. 1.4 for the roles of involved experts, e.g., the product manager as a domain expert.

Model-based reasoning, or more broadly Knowledge Representation and Reasoning (KRR), belongs to "traditional", i.e., symbolic AI techniques that have been developed over several decades [60]. Currently, sub-symbolic or data-driven AI is much more popular. However, they have limitations such as a lack of reliability, limited reasoning abilities, and a lack of specialized knowledge in general-purpose LLMs. These limitations are highly relevant for product configuration, as the correctness of the results is especially important. Therefore, LLMs alone cannot replace traditional configuration engines. However, a combination of both (i.e., hybrid AI) can help (see Chap. 8).

Symbolic AI techniques are able to solve hard problems, but they typically have weaknesses with large problems even if they are easy (i.e., potential time-outs due to exponential growth caused by the inherent NP-hardness [31]). Therefore, a good product configurator needs both powerful AI techniques and domain-specific extensions or alternatives such as heuristics.[4]

In the following sections, we give brief introductions into the relevant technologies. For more details, please refer to the referenced works. Finally, a brief remark on choosing between these technologies: Naturally, there is no one-size-fits-all solution. Each of the presented technologies has its own strengths and weaknesses, and we can only give very rough guidance on how to choose one. Variant tables, decision diagrams, and feature models are representations that are very easily understandable (by humans) when they are small. For practical implementations that exceed a certain size, usually other technologies are used. Rule-based systems can demonstrate their advantages when purely declarative approaches don't perform well enough, but they come with the cost of lower maintainability. Logic-based approaches lend themselves very well to combinatorial or object-oriented problems, while constraint programming excels for problems with large (e.g., numeric) domains.

## 5.1  Variant Tables and Decision Diagrams

For a long time, tables or spreadsheets have been used for product configuration. This is because they have many advantages: There is no special expertise needed; they provide a good overview of the dependencies, explicitly represent compatibilities or incompatibilities, and are usable for automated processing. Tables are the standard form for extensional data representation in business; they are widespread due to the success of Microsoft Excel and similar tools.

Unfortunately, tables have disadvantages as well. It is impossible to encode complicated dependencies; typically only one-to-one incompatibilities are supported. Dependencies might be represented redundantly. Complexity can easily be underestimated at the beginning, causing high development effort later on. If formulas are

---

[4] See Chap. 7 for some concrete ideas.

used, maintenance becomes much more expensive because knowledge evolution will require code changes. It is quite difficult to ensure quality because regression testing is difficult.[5]

Variant tables are a special form of tables that build upon their advantages and improve them by compressing redundant information. Standard tables enumerate all variants of a product explicitly. This becomes problematic if the number of possible variants for valid configurations exceeds the number of potential customers. This can be the case very soon if we consider the exponential growth of variants. To address this issue, c-tuples have been introduced for compression in variant tables. We refer to the work by Albert Haag and Laura Haag [39] for more details. See Table 5.1 and the corresponding text for an example (our folding bike).

Variant tables can be translated to (Binary) Decision Diagrams [1], but the latter can also be modeled directly: as a graph of decision points where each branch (yes or no) leads to the next decisions. One advantage of decision diagrams is that they can be pre-compiled to make configurator user interfaces very responsive. Disadvantages are that they are not suitable for very large products and that constraints are represented only implicitly.

Several configuration system vendors use these technologies: Variant tables are used, e.g., in SAP systems [8], and Configit implements decision diagrams [40].

## 5.2  Feature Models

Features are a natural way of describing any product: Each feature adds a unique distinction and can be seen as an increment of product functionality [5]. Feature modeling (FM) [44] is a formal approach to model configurable products in terms of their features. There are easily understandable visual and text-based languages for FM, there are tools that support them, and FMs can be mapped to ASP, CSP, and SAT (cf. Sects. 5.4 and 5.5).

We recommend the book *Feature Models: AI-driven Design, Analysis, and Applications* by Alexander Felfernig, Andreas Falkner, and David Benavides [26] (especially Chap. 2 and Sect. 5.2) to learn about feature models.

Feature models have several advantages: No special expertise is needed to model and understand them; they provide a good overview of the product structure (in the form of a tree); they are standardized (Feature-oriented Domain Analysis—FODA [44]); they provide useful metrics (e.g., number of solutions, mandatory and dead features); and pre-compilation makes configurator user interfaces very fast.

Feature models have disadvantages as well: they are not suitable for very large products, and complicated dependencies and sub-part structures are difficult to encode.

Figure 5.5 in the Example section below shows how to represent the folding bike example from Fig. 3.5 as a feature model.

---

[5] The same disadvantages also hold for programmed or scripting approaches.

## 5.3  Rule-Based Systems

Rule-based systems have a very long history[6] and are used by several tools because they are easy to handle and to understand. The main technology involves rules in the form of "if A then B", often together with a simple, deterministic way of reasoning: forward chaining (i.e., if A becomes valid then B is also derived).[7]

This approach combines the advantages of being model-based (due to separation of knowledge—in the form of rules—and processing by forward chaining) and efficient (due to the search-avoiding execution that simply tries to match the antecedent and derive the consequent) [53]. The processing order (i.e., which of several matching rules is executed first) may influence the result: For example, given the two rules "if A then C=1" and "if B then C=2", setting A and B together may result in either 1 or 2 as value for C. Such situations are difficult to debug and maintain.

Thinking in terms of consequences is natural for humans and therefore easy to understand. However, it lacks an explicit representation of product structure (i.e., a sub-part tree) and undirected data dependencies such as $A = B$ (which leads to duplicated code, i.e., two rules for one constraint). Complexity can easily be underestimated at the beginning, causing high development effort later on (see Foreword and Chap. 2 in [28]).

Many systems allow complex computations or side-effects (e.g., error messages like in the example for rule-based systems towards the end of this chapter) in the then-part – similar to procedural programming or scripting. This makes maintenance much more expensive because knowledge evolution will require code changes. It is quite difficult to ensure quality because regression testing is difficult.

## 5.4  Logic-Based Approaches

In this section, we take a very short look at various logics and how they can be used for product configuration. We start with basic concepts of logics and briefly mention several approaches built on top of them, and afterward focus on one approach in detail: Answer Set Programming (ASP).

---

[6] Going back to expert systems, such as MYCIN, in the 1960s [30].

[7] On the other hand, if B is known to be false then one can derive that A cannot be valid as well (based on the logical meaning of implications). Therefore, one rule can be used in two directions. This is, however, still less powerful than arbitrary constraints. For example, with the constraint $2 \times A = B$ (the value of variable B is twice the value of A), $B$ can be computed given the value of $A$, and $A$ can also be computed given the value of $B$.

## SAT Solving and Other Logic-Based Approaches

Propositional logic [12, 60] (comprising Boolean variables and expressions) is the simplest logic that can be used for product configuration. The Boolean variables represent the features or the product properties, and the constraints are coded as Boolean expressions. Variables and Boolean expressions can be created directly for a given configuration problem or generated from a higher-level formalism such as feature models (cf. Sect. 5.2) [26].

SAT (satisfiability) solvers are powerful tools for solving such representations in propositional logic [29, 61]. Advanced variants called *SAT modulo theories* (SMT) [4] extend pure Boolean reasoning with integer and floating-point numbers or with temporal or spatial constraints. Higher-order logics such as Datalog [11], Answer Set Programming (ASP), or Alloy [23] are based on first-order logic to more easily define a configuration problem.

Since logics are very well-suited to specify configuration problems and support solving them, logic-based approaches form the basis of many applications in the area of product configuration. This section presents a small selection of relevant approaches.

COOM[8] [6, 59] is a language for product configuration knowledge bases that can be translated into ASP.

Another form of higher-order logics are Description Logics (DL) [27, 48]. *Shapes Constraint Language* (SHACL) is a standardized add-on for DL that enables constraints to be defined. Tool support for SHACL is currently restricted to checking constraints instead of solving them. Description Logics easily lend themselves to integration with knowledge graphs [41] for definition of configuration problems similarly to feature models.

## Answer Set Programming

Logic programming [60] is a declarative approach in which the declarative model consists of logical sentences and the solvers implement efficient reasoning algorithms. Prolog is a logic programming language that has been in wide use since the 1970s, was standardized in 1995 [42], and has been used for product configuration [25].

The currently predominant approach to logic programming is Answer Set Programming (ASP) [3, 10, 34, 36, 47], its syntax resembles Prolog's. ASP is a declarative knowledge representation formalism applied successfully in many industrial and scientific applications [20, 22].

The general idea is to model a problem specification, utilize domain-independent solving algorithms to solve it, and obtain solutions to the original problem by interpreting the models computed by the solver (cf. Fig. 5.4, note the similarity to

---

[8] https://www.coom-lang.org/, https://github.com/potassco/coom-suite.

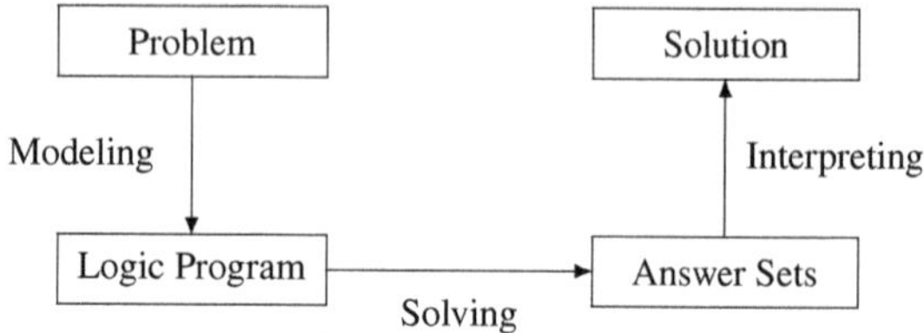

**Fig. 5.4** Using ASP to solve a problem (slightly adapted from Potassco's teaching materials [55])



Fig. 1.4). In ASP, the problem specification takes the form of a *logic program*, i.e., a set of first-order rules[9] that may contain variables. The models computed by the solver are called *answer sets*.

In product configuration, one typical *Problem* referred to in Fig. 5.4 is finding a valid configuration, where the *Logic Program* specifies the product model and all constraints. The solver computes one or more *Answer Sets* encoding the valid configurations (or none, if there is no solution), which can be interpreted and transformed into actual configurations.

One software system that can solve (i.e., find solutions for) logic programs encoded in ASP is CLINGO[10] [33].

ASP is based on first-order logic (FOL) and thus benefits from FOL's focus on two important real-world concepts: objects and relations. By being able to represent just these two concepts, FOL, and thus ASP, allows for the representation of a good deal of everyday knowledge. For example, to express that a saddle is a part of a bike, we just write `part_of(saddle,bike)`: `saddle` is a constant term referring to the real-world object "saddle", `bike` represents the bike, and `part_of` is a predicate referring to the real-world relation where one object is part of another. Unary predicates are used to represent properties of objects; e.g., `electric(bike001)` states that the object identified as `bike001` is *electric*. Predicates of higher arity are used to represent relations between several objects, such as the example above. The arity of predicates is not limited but needs to be finite.[11]

This introduction to ASP syntax is both simplified and brief. See [32, 35, 47] for details. For example, we omit here the powerful feature of first-order variables, which are used to concisely express general rules about arbitrary sets of objects. These first-order variables are also the cause of a prominent issue of ASP, the *grounding bottleneck* [22], which makes solving large problems challenging. Another powerful feature is optimization, which can be used to find a configuration that fulfills some optimality criteria (such as $CO_2$ emissions or cost).

---

[9] Here, the term "rule" has a meaning different from that in Sects. 5.3, where we focus on the deterministic and procedural execution of rules. For ASP, it is simply a syntactic form that comprises logical facts, implications, and constraints.

[10] https://potassco.org/clingo/.

[11] Putting bounds on predicate arities can provide certain guarantees on solving complexity, though [19].

ASP has been used to reason about object-oriented configuration problems[12] [2, 13, 16, 24], feature models [52], or other logical representations of configuration problems [58]. Improving ASP's solving performance for large-scale configuration problems is an active area of research [14, 15].

In Listing 5.1 below we show how to encode the folding bike example in ASP.

## 5.5  Constraint Programming

Constraint Programming (CP) [57, 60] is another well-known approach to knowledge-based reasoning. A Constraint Satisfaction Problem (CSP) consists of a set of decision variables, their respective domains, and a set of constraints. In contrast to imperative programming, variables are not assigned values through assignment statements in an algorithm, but their value is *decided* by a solver. Given a CSP, the solver's task is to compute an assignment of exactly one value for each decision variable, such that the value of each variable is included in its domain and satisfies all the constraints. Constraint Programming has been successfully used as an underlying technique for product configuration for several decades [21, 43, 63]. Like ASP, constraint programming supports optimization, e.g., to find optimal configurations.

For example, in the folding bike example (see the PLM view in Fig. 3.5 and the CRM view in Fig. 3.6), the `Seat`'s `seatpost` attribute could be modeled by a decision variable *seat.seatpost* that has the domain {*standard*, *extended*, *telescope*}. The `customer_height` attribute from the CRM view, on the other hand, could be modeled by a variable *customer_height*, with the integer range 150..200 as domain. Corresponding constraints (in pseudocode) would then look as follows (cf. the section on CRM/Sales View in the Example in Chap. 3):

- *seat.seatpost* = "standard" $\implies$ *customer_height* $\leq$ 180
- *seat.seatpost* = "extended" $\implies$ *customer_height* $\in$ 177..189
- *seat.seatpost* = "telescope" $\implies$ *customer_height* > 185.

Compared to rules (cf. Sect. 5.3), constraints are more powerful: For example, with the constraint $2 \times A = B$ (the value of variable B is twice the value of A), $B$ can be computed given the value of $A$, and also $A$ can be computed given the value of $B$. Powerful solving algorithms have been developed that find solutions to sets of such constraints efficiently, and we do not have to consider the processing order when designing constraints. On the other hand, rules can be more efficient than constraint solving, because the directed evaluation of rules avoids search.

One popular language and family of systems for CP is MINIZINC[13] [49, 54, 65, 66]. MiniZinc is a high-level constraint modeling language that is compiled into the lower-level language of FlatZinc. FlatZinc can be processed by various solvers,

---

[12] Results from this research are known as OOASP, cf. https://github.com/siemens/OOASP.

[13] https://www.minizinc.org/.

including Constraint Programming solvers (such as Gecode[14] [64], Chuffed,[15] or OR-Tools[16]) and Mixed-Integer Programming solvers (such as Gurobi[17]).

Other popular CP systems and libraries include Choco[18] [56] (for Java), OR-Tools[19] (for various programming languages), and CPMPy[20] [37] (for Python), among many others.

There have been attempts to develop more elaborate, generic encodings and/or to extend the MiniZinc language itself, aiming to support the definition of object-oriented (configuration) problems [63, 67]. Most recently, Tack et al. [67] have suggested an extension of the MiniZinc language that is very close to UML class diagrams and supports decision variables of object type, objects referring to other objects, and variable sets of objects whose cardinality is decided by the solver.

In Listing 5.2 below we show how to encode the folding bike example in MiniZinc.

## 5.6  Commercial Products

Commercial configurators use a range of different technologies. We cannot provide a comprehensive overview here, as there are hundreds or perhaps even thousands of tools, and the market evolves constantly.

For example, Oracle had a very strong configurator and acquired several competitors over the years. These developments and acquisitions resulted in Oracle's current offering, Oracle CPQ,[21] which is a cloud-based configure-price-quote (CPQ) solution.

Similarly, SAP [38] combined decades of its own developments with acquisitions and is currently offering SAP CPQ[22] as their cloud solution. For the classical use-cases they have switched to the new SAP AVC (Advanced Variant Configurator) [9] which is completely constraint-based and is intended to replace their widely used LO-VC variant configurator over the next few years.[23]

Siemens' Teamcenter[24] is a PLM solution that includes a configurator based on a so-called 150% configuration—a type of product variant master that describes

---

[14] https://www.gecode.dev/.

[15] https://github.com/chuffed/chuffed.

[16] https://developers.google.com/optimization/.

[17] https://www.gurobi.com.

[18] https://choco-solver.org/.

[19] https://developers.google.com/optimization/.

[20] https://github.com/CPMpy/cpmpy.

[21] https://www.oracle.com/cx/sales/cpq/.

[22] https://www.sap.com/products/financial-management/cpq.html.

[23] This example demonstrates the challenges of new tooling in general: Customers hesitate to migrate due to the potentially involved efforts and risks—even though SAP kept the interfaces of AVC and LO-VC very similar to allow for smooth migrations.

[24] https://plm.sw.siemens.com/en-US/teamcenter/.

the entire product with the idea of filtering from this overall model the variants a customer needs, which are then so-called 100% configurations. Rulestream[25] is a complementary system for engineer-to-order configuration (i.e., large and complex systems). The great advantage is that all these systems have excellent integration into their CAD systems and simulators. So it's quite easy to configure a product and to simulate its function as well as its manufacturing (in a factory that is also configured and designed in Teamcenter) and to use this information to improve the product.

While such tools are well integrated into the other offerings of these companies, many vendors offer stand-alone solutions. Just to mention a few examples in alphabetical order: Camos,[26] CAS Merlin,[27] Configit,[28] encoway,[29] and Tacton[30] have strong adoption in Europe. These systems use different technologies like tables, rules, constraints, or decision diagrams, and they typically have different strengths and weaknesses. Some concentrate on or integrate CAD tools, others focus on small and medium-sized enterprises, some are very strong in the cloud, others offer very good constraint solvers, and so on.

There used to be a system whose solver was based on Answer Set Programming (ASP), VariSales [69], but it has since changed to a constraint-based approach [70].

For a structured presentation and business-focused comparison of currently available tools, we recommend the Gartner Magic Quadrant for Configure, Price and Quote Applications [46], Gartner's online catalogue of CPQ applications reviews and ratings,[31] and the Forrester Wave report on CPQ Solutions [51].

For a specific configuration problem or configurable product, the question always arises which tool to select. The bad news is that there is no one-size-fits-all solution. No single tool will fit all user requirements. We recommend analyzing the requirements for each concrete use case and comparing various vendors against them. For some ideas how to define such requirements and find a fitting vendor, see also Chap. 7 and especially Fig. 7.3. For a shortlist of 2–3 promising candidates, a prototypical proof of concept can then provide a clear picture of which system to continue with for a larger project and finally move into operational use.

---

[25] https://www.plm.automation.siemens.com/global/en/products/collaboration/rulestream-engineer-to-order.html.

[26] https://www.camos.de.

[27] https://www.cas-merlin.de.

[28] https://configit.com.

[29] https://www.encoway.de.

[30] https://www.tacton.com.

[31] https://www.gartner.com/reviews/market/configure-price-quote-applications.

# Example

## *Variant Table*

Table 5.1 is a variant table for the folding bike example in Chap. 3, comprising the product data (Fig. 3.5) and the customer requirements (Fig. 3.6). There are many other representations (e.g., different grouping or ordering) to achieve the same result.

Each column of a table represents a configurable entity. In this table, the first three columns represent the user requirements; the other columns represent product properties. Different types are supported: Boolean (e.g., offroad or mudguard), enumerations (e.g., frame material or seatpost), and numbers (e.g., customer height). Here we modeled the reflectors of the two wheels in one column (similar to the mudguards) because that directly reflects the intent (i.e., either both wheels have reflectors or both do not) and avoids having to implement the corresponding constraint.

Each row of the table represents allowed combinations. For a compact representation, we allow multiple values for columns, separated by commas, and numerical ranges, such as 150–176. The first row expresses that a customer height between 150 and 176 with no preference for off-road and vegan, a regular folding bike without a motor and battery, a standard seatpost, and any frame material (i.e., steel or titanium), saddle material, and mudguard and reflector presence (i.e., yes or no) is valid. We use "*" as a shortcut for all values of a column (i.e., those occurring in any other row). The set of all rows defines all valid products – all other combinations of values are invalid.

As can be seen, however, the size of variant tables tends to explode despite these compactifications. The same value combinations occur repeatedly in the table. The reason is that several subsets of columns are independent from the others. The table can be split into several smaller tables (similar to normalization in relational databases) that represent the underlying constraints:[32]

1. height, seatpost
2. offroad, mudguards
3. type, motor, battery
4. vegan, saddle
5. frame[33]
6. reflectors.

Such smaller constraint tables are easier to maintain and can be automatically combined into the large variant table [39].

---

[32] Here, the columns of the smaller tables do not overlap. If we had more constraints, they could overlap.

[33] We use single columns as unary constraints: Just to define the value domain. These values are not dependent on other columns, and any of them can be selected.

**Table 5.1**  A variant table for the folding bike (abbreviations: offroad, mudguards, reflectors)

| Height | Offr | Vegan | Type | Motor | Battery | Frame | Mudg | Saddle | Seatpost | Ref |
|---|---|---|---|---|---|---|---|---|---|---|
| 150–176 | No | No | Regular | No | No | Steel, titanium | Yes, No | Synthetic, leather | Standard | Yes, No |
| 150–176 | No | Yes | Regular | No | No | * | * | Synthetic | Standard | * |
| 150–176 | Yes | No | Regular | No | No | * | Yes | * | Standard | * |
| 150–176 | Yes | Yes | Regular | No | No | * | Yes | Synthetic | Standard | * |
| 177–180 | No | No | Regular | No | No | * | * | * | Standard, extended | * |
| 177–180 | No | Yes | Regular | No | No | * | * | Synthetic | Standard, extended | * |
| 177–180 | Yes | No | Regular | No | No | * | Yes | * | Standard, extended | * |
| 177–180 | Yes | Yes | Regular | No | No | * | Yes | Synthetic | Standard, extended | * |
| 181–185 | No | No | Regular | No | No | * | * | * | Extended | * |
| 181–185 | No | Yes | Regular | No | No | * | * | Synthetic | Extended | * |
| 181–185 | Yes | No | Regular | No | No | * | Yes | * | Extended | * |
| 181–185 | Yes | Yes | Regular | No | No | * | Yes | Synthetic | Extended | * |
| 186–189 | No | No | Regular | No | No | * | * | * | Extended, telescope | * |
| 186–189 | No | Yes | Regular | No | No | * | * | Synthetic | Extended, telescope | * |
| 186–189 | Yes | No | Regular | No | No | * | Yes | * | Extended, telescope | * |
| 186–189 | Yes | Yes | Regular | No | No | * | Yes | Synthetic | Extended, telescope | * |
| 190–200 | No | No | Regular | No | No | * | * | * | Telescope | * |
| 190–200 | No | Yes | Regular | No | No | * | * | Synthetic | Telescope | * |
| 190–200 | Yes | No | Regular | No | No | * | Yes | * | Telescope | * |
| 190–200 | Yes | Yes | Regular | No | No | * | Yes | Synthetic | Telescope | * |
| 150–176 | No | No | Electric | Yes | Yes | * | * | * | Standard | * |
| 150–176 | No | Yes | Electric | Yes | Yes | * | * | Synthetic | Standard | * |
| 150–176 | Yes | No | Electric | Yes | Yes | * | Yes | * | Standard | * |

(continued)

**Table 5.1** (continued)

| Height | Offr | Vegan | Type | Motor | Battery | Frame | Mudg | Saddle | Seatpost | Ref |
|---|---|---|---|---|---|---|---|---|---|---|
| 150–176 | Yes | Yes | Electric | Yes | Yes | * | Yes | Synthetic | Standard | * |
| 177–180 | No | No | Electric | Yes | Yes | * | * | * | Standard, extended | * |
| 177–180 | No | Yes | Electric | Yes | Yes | * | * | Synthetic | Standard, extended | * |
| 177–180 | Yes | No | Electric | Yes | Yes | * | Yes | * | Standard, extended | * |
| 177–180 | Yes | Yes | Electric | Yes | Yes | * | Yes | Synthetic | Standard, extended | * |
| 181–185 | No | No | Electric | Yes | Yes | * | * | * | Extended | * |
| 181–185 | No | Yes | Electric | Yes | Yes | * | * | Synthetic | Extended | * |
| 181–185 | Yes | No | Electric | Yes | Yes | * | Yes | * | Extended | * |
| 181–185 | Yes | Yes | Electric | Yes | Yes | * | Yes | Synthetic | Extended | * |
| 186–189 | No | No | Electric | Yes | Yes | * | * | * | Extended, telescope | * |
| 186–189 | No | Yes | Electric | Yes | Yes | * | * | Synthetic | Extended, telescope | * |
| 186–189 | Yes | No | Electric | Yes | Yes | * | Yes | * | Extended, telescope | * |
| 186–189 | Yes | Yes | Electric | Yes | Yes | * | Yes | Synthetic | Extended, telescope | * |
| 190–200 | No | No | Electric | Yes | Yes | * | * | * | Telescope | * |
| 190–200 | No | Yes | Electric | Yes | Yes | * | * | Synthetic | Telescope | * |
| 190–200 | Yes | No | Electric | Yes | Yes | * | Yes | * | Telescope | * |
| 190–200 | Yes | Yes | Electric | Yes | Yes | * | Yes | Synthetic | Telescope | * |

## *Feature Model*

Figure 5.5 shows the folding bike example from Fig. 3.5 as a feature model. The root feature, representing the entire product, is `FoldingBike`. Arcs connect features to their sub-features. Solid dots signify *mandatory* features (e.g., each `Frame` must contain a `FrameMaterial`), while hollow dots signify *optional* features (e.g., each `Frame` may or may not contain `Mudguards`). Arcs connected by a horizontal line signify *alternatives*; e.g., a `FrameMaterial` is either `SteelFrame` or `TitaniumFrame` but not both. The arrows between `FrontReflectors` and `BackReflectors` signify *cross-tree constraints* that mean each of the two features *requires* the other.

This example illustrates that the FM formalism does not lend itself very well to complex object-oriented configuration problems: Subclasses `RegularFoldingBike` and `ElectricFoldingBike` have to be modeled as features, which is as unintuitive as modeling `Motor` and `Battery` as sub-features of the `Electric` type. An alternative approach for this aspect would be to model `Motor` and `Battery` as features of `FoldingBike` and add appropriate cross-tree constraints.

In a standard feature model, the two wheels have to be modeled separately, introducing some redundancy (which is acceptable for two wheels but would not be feasible for components with higher potential cardinalities). Sub-features of `FrontWheel` and `BackWheel` have different names in this FM to make them distinguishable. Two "requires" constraints ensure that both wheels are configured in the same way.

Cardinality-based Feature Models [17] have a higher expressiveness than standard FMs. They allow for the specification of numbers (cardinalities) of multiple features. For the folding bike, we can define that it has exactly two sub-features for wheels. Thus, we need not specify `FrontWheel` and `BackWheel`, but only `Wheel` with

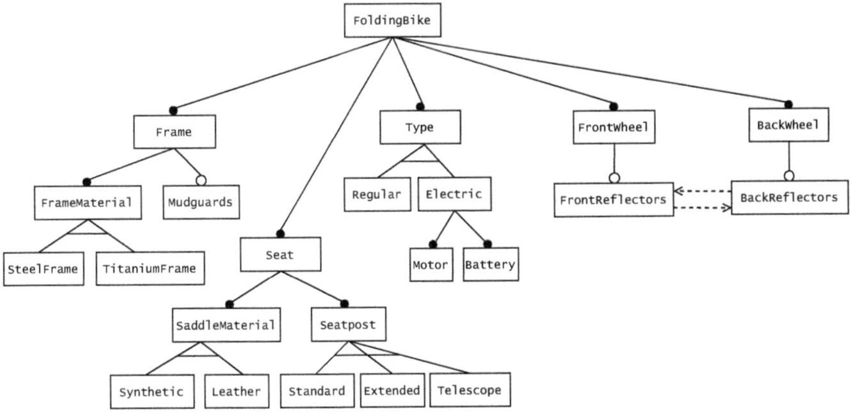

**Fig. 5.5** The folding bike example from Fig. 3.5 as an FM (*Source* own work)

a cardinality of 2. The different instances can be configured differently. Therefore, we still need a constraint that the values for their reflectors must be equal.

## *Rule-Based*

Rule-based configurators typically present a sequence of decisions to the user; see DOPLER[34] as an example [18]. For our folding bike example from Chap. 3, we extracted the following decision variables for the user interface:

- *height*: 150–200 cm
- *offroad*: yes, no
- *vegan*: yes, no
- *electric*: yes, no
- *mudguards*: yes, no
- *reflectors*: yes, no
- *material*: steel, titanium
- *saddle*: synthetic, leather
- *seatpost*: standard, extended, telescope.

The user can decide about customer requirements (from Fig. 3.6, the first three in the list above) and relevant product data (from Fig. 3.5). We hide the motor and battery from the user because they are covered by the decision for electric (see the first two rules below). Furthermore, we do not allow separately selecting the reflectors for the front and back wheel, thus avoiding explicitly implementing the constraint that both must be the same. There is a rule that off-road usage requires mudguards, but mudguards can also be selected if off-road is not. Finally, we show an example of side-effect rules: If the seatpost does not match the customer's height, then an error message is shown. Here is the list of all rules:

- if *electric* then *motor*
- if *electric* then *battery*
- if *offroad* then *mudguards*
- if *height* < 177 and *seatpost* = extended then error
- if *height* > 180 and *seatpost* = standard then error
- if *height* < 186 and *seatpost* = telescope then error
- if *height* > 189 and *seatpost* = extended then error.

---

[34] https://ase.jku.at/dopler/.

## *Answer Set Programming*

The folding bike example from Chap. 3, comprising the customer requirements (Fig. 3.6) and the product data (Fig. 3.5), can be encoded in ASP as follows:

```
1   % PLM / Engineering view:
2
3   foldingbike.
4   { electric } :- foldingbike.
5   motor :- electric.
6   battery :- electric.
7   frame :- foldingbike.
8   material(steel); material(titanium) :- frame.
9   { mudguards } :- frame.
10  seat :- foldingbike.
11  saddle_material(synthetic);
        saddle_material(leather) :- seat.
12  seatpost(standard); seatpost(extended);
        seatpost(telescope) :- seat.
13  wheel(1..2) :- foldingbike.
14  reflectors(W,true); reflectors(W,false) :-
        wheel(W).
15
16  % constraint - two wheels must be configured in
        the same way:
17  :- reflectors(W1,true), reflectors(W2,false).
18
19  % CRM / Sales view:
20
21  { customer_height(H) : H = 150..200 } = 1.
22  { offroad }.
23  { vegan }.
24
25  % constraints:
26  :- customer_height(H), H > 180,
        seatpost(standard).
27  :- customer_height(H), H > 189,
        seatpost(extended).
28  :- customer_height(H), H < 177,
        seatpost(extended).
29  :- customer_height(H), H <= 185,
        seatpost(telescope).
30  :- offroad, not mudguards.
31  :- vegan, saddle_material(leather).
```

**Listing 5.1** ASP encoding of part of the folding bike example

This encoding uses choice rules (e.g., `{customer_height(H) : H = 150..200 } = 1.` means that the customer's height must have exactly one value between 150 and 200), constraints (e.g., `:- offroad, not mudguards.` means that it may not be the case that `offroad` is true while `mudguards` is not true), disjunction (encoded by a semicolon), and other features. For more detailed explanations of these and other features of ASP, we refer to the Potassco Guide [32].

## *Constraint Programming*

The folding bike example from Chapter 3, comprising the customer requirements (Fig. 3.6) and the product data (Fig. 3.5), can be encoded in MiniZinc as follows:

```
1  % PLM / Engineering view:
2
3  enum FrameMaterialType = {steel, titanium};
4  var FrameMaterialType: frame_material;
5
6  var bool: mudguards;
7
8  enum SaddleMaterialType = {synthetic, leather};
9  var SaddleMaterialType: saddle_material;
10
11 enum SeatpostType = {standard, extended,
       telescope};
12 var SeatpostType: seatpost;
13
14 array[1..2] of var bool: wheel_reflectors;
15
16 include "all_equal.mzn";
17 constraint all_equal(wheel_reflectors);
18
19 enum FoldingBikeType = {regular, electric};
20 var FoldingBikeType: foldingbike_type;
21
22 var bool: motor;
23 var bool: battery;
24
25 constraint (foldingbike_type = electric)
26             <-> (motor /\ battery);
27
28 % CRM / Sales view:
29
30 par 150..200: customer_height;
31 par bool: offroad;
32 par bool: vegan;
33
34 constraint customer_height > 180 -> seatpost !=
       standard;
35 constraint not (customer_height in 177..189)
36             -> seatpost != extended;
37 constraint customer_height <= 185 -> seatpost !=
       telescope;
38 constraint offroad -> mudguards;
39 constraint vegan -> saddle_material != leather;
```

**Listing 5.2**  MiniZinc encoding of part of the folding bike example

This encoding uses enumerated domains, an integer domain, an `all_equal` constraint, implications in constraints, and other features of the MiniZinc language. For detailed explanations of these and further concepts, we refer to the MiniZinc Handbook [65].

## Exercises

**Exercise 5.1** Model the regular folding bike from Fig. 3.5 (without any constraints) as a feature model in SPLOT [50],[35] FeatureIDE,[36] or another feature modeling tool.

Reflect on the design choices you make during modeling. What do you have to do differently than with UML, for example?

**Exercise 5.2** Extend your feature model from Sect. 5.1, modeling the two wheels as separate features. Furthermore, add features to represent two types of wheels (marathon, urban). Add cross-tree constraints that ensure that the two wheels are equal. Furthermore, add the constraint that marathon wheels exclude mudguards.

How many valid configurations are there?

Configure two variants of the product (one with marathon wheels, one with urban wheels) with SPLOT's configurator.

**Exercise 5.3** Run the ASP and MiniZinc encodings given in this chapter with CLINGO[37] (or another ASP system), or with MINIZINC[38] (or another CP system).

How many valid configurations are there?

**Exercise 5.4** Encode the complete PLM/Engineering view on the folding bike example from Fig. 3.5 (including the constraints on the wheels) in OOASP [24]. Make sure you can use a solver to complete a partial configuration specified by you.

Use the "old OOASP encodings"[39] for this task. You can use the given racks example as inspiration.

**Exercise 5.5** Encode the complete PLM/Engineering view on the folding bike example from Fig. 3.5 (including the constraints on the wheels) in OOCSP [63] or in MiniZinc with Objects [67]. Make sure you can use a solver to complete a partial configuration specified by you.

If you do OOCSP, use the provided OOCSP encodings[40] for this task. You can use the given racks example as inspiration.

---

[35] http://www.splot-research.org/.

[36] https://featureide.github.io/.

[37] https://potassco.org/clingo/.

[38] https://www.minizinc.org/.

[39] https://github.com/siemens/OOASP/tree/main/old_encodings.

[40] https://github.com/siemens/OOCSP/blob/master/2016_CWS/oocsp1.mzn.

**Exercise 5.6**  The current implementation of OOASP[41] provides a clinguin-based UI [7] for interactive configuration. Adapt your OOASP encoding of the folding bike example (at least the complete PLM view) for this version of OOASP, and experiment with the UI to load the knowledge base, interactively create configurations, etc. Prepare a demonstration of the UI that includes all relevant features.

**Exercise 5.7**  Extend a working ASP encoding of the folding bike example (does not need to be OOASP) by an ERP/Parts view like in Fig. 3.7 and Table 3.1 (but, of course, with complete data for all components and several suppliers). Find out how to use optimization statements and/or weak constraints[42] in ASP and use them to configure a folding bike satisfying various customer requirements at minimal cost. Then, add a second objective variable (e.g., carbon footprint) to the ERP/Parts view and explore how to use $\texttt{asprin}$[43] for Pareto optimization.

**Exercise 5.8**  Extend a working MiniZinc encoding of the folding bike example (does not need to be OOCSP) by an ERP/Parts view like in Fig. 3.7 and Table 3.1 (but, of course, with complete data for all components and several suppliers). Find out how to use optimization statements[44] in MiniZinc and use them to configure a folding bike satisfying various customer requirements at minimal cost.

**Exercise 5.9**  Model the bicycle (user requirements and product offering) from Sect. 4.6 as far as possible and reasonable

- with variant tables
- as a feature model
- in a rule-based way
- in ASP (or OOASP)
- in MiniZinc (classical or the new object syntax [67])
- with any other approach you find convenient.

Reflect on the suitability of these technologies for your product model.

# References


1. Akers, S.: Binary decision diagrams. IEEE Trans. Comput. **27**(6), 509–516 (1978)
2. Balážová, L., Comploi-Taupe, R., Hahn, S., Rühling, N., Schenner, G.: Smart expansion techniques for ASP-based interactive configuration. Theory Pract. Log. Program. (2025). https://doi.org/10.1017/S147106842510029X
3. Baral, C.: Knowledge Representation: Reasoning and Declarative Problem Solving. Cambridge University Press, Cambridge (2003)


---

[41] https://github.com/siemens/OOASP.

[42] see, for example, Sect. 11.1 in the Potassco Guide version 2.2.0 [32].

[43] https://potassco.org/asprin/; see, for example, Sect. 11.2 in the Potassco Guide version 2.2.0 [32].

[44] see, for example, Sect. 2.1.2 in the MiniZinc Handbook [65].

4. Barrett, C.W., Sebastiani, R., Seshia, S.A., Tinelli, C.: Satisfiability modulo theories. In: Biere, A., Heule, M., van Maaren, H., Walsh, T. (eds.) Handbook of Satisfiability, 2nd edn, Frontiers in Artificial Intelligence and Applications, vol. 336, pp. 1267–1329. IOS Press (2021). https://doi.org/10.3233/FAIA201017

5. Batory, D.: Feature models, grammars, and propositional formulas. In: Obbink, H., Pohl, K. (eds.) International Conference on Software Product Lines, pp. 7–20. Springer, Berlin Heidelberg, Berlin, Heidelberg (2005). https://doi.org/10.1007/11554844_3

6. Baumeister, J., Herud, K., Ostrowski, M., Reutelshöfer, J., Rühling, N., Schaub, T., Wanko, P.: Towards industrial-scale product configuration. In: Dodaro, C., Gupta, G., Martinez, M.V. (eds.) Logic Programming and Nonmonotonic Reasoning - 17th International Conference, LPNMR 2024, Dallas, TX, USA, October 11–14, 2024, Proceedings, Lecture Notes in Computer Science, vol. 15245, pp. 71–84. Springer (2024). https://doi.org/10.1007/978-3-031-74209-5_6

7. Beiser, A., Hahn, S., Schaub, T.: ASP-driven user-interaction with Clinguin. In: Cabalar, P., Fabiano, F., Gebser, M., Gupta, G., Swift, T. (eds.) Proceedings 40th International Conference on Logic Programming, ICLP 2024, University of Texas at Dallas, Dallas Texas, USA, October 14–17 2024, EPTCS, vol. 416, pp. 215–228 (2024). https://doi.org/10.4204/EPTCS.416.19

8. Blumöhr, U., Münch, M., Ukalovic, M.: Variant Configuration with SAP, 2nd edn. SAP PRESS (2011)

9. Blumöhr, U., Kölbl, A., Neuhaus, M., Ukalovic, M.: Advanced variant configuration in SAP S/4HANA. Rheinwerk Publishing (2023)

10. Brewka, G., Eiter, T., Truszczynski, M.: Answer set programming at a glance. Commun. ACM 54(12), 92–103 (2011). https://doi.org/10.1145/2043174.2043195

11. Ceri, S., Gottlob, G., Tanca, L.: Syntax and semantics of Datalog. In: Logic Programming and Databases, pp. 77–93. Springer, Berlin Heidelberg, Berlin, Heidelberg (1990). https://doi.org/10.1007/978-3-642-83952-8-6

12. Chang, C.L., Lee, R.C.T.: Symbolic Logic and Mechanical Theorem Proving. Academic press (1973)

13. Comploi-Taupe, R., Falkner, A., Hahn, S., Schaub, T., Schenner, G.: Interactive configuration with ASP multi-shot solving. In: Horcas, J., Galindo, J., Comploi-Taupe, R., Fuentes, L. (eds.) Proceedings of the Twenty-fifth International Configuration Workshop (CONF'23), vol. 3509, pp. 95–103. CEUR Workshop Proceedings (2023). https://ceur-ws.org/Vol-3509/paper13.pdf

14. Comploi-Taupe, R., Francescutto, G., Schenner, G.: Applying incremental answer set solving to product configuration. In: Felfernig, A., Fuentes, L., Cleland-Huang, J., Assunção, W.K.G., Quinton, C., Guo, J., Schmid, K., Huchard, M., Ayala, I., Rojas, J.M., Le, V., Horcas, J.M. (eds.) SPLC '22: 26th ACM International Systems and Software Product Line Conference, Graz, Austria, September 12–16, 2022, Vol. B, pp. 150–155. ACM (2022). https://doi.org/10.1145/3503229.3547069

15. Comploi-Taupe, R., Friedrich, G., Schekotihin, K., Weinzierl, A.: Domain-specific heuristics in answer set programming: a declarative non-monotonic approach. J. Artif. Intell. Res. 76, 59–114 (2023). https://doi.org/10.1613/JAIR.1.14091

16. Comploi-Taupe, R., Hahn, S., Schenner, G., Schaub, T.: Challenges of developing an API for interactive configuration using ASP. In: Tarzariol, A., Laferrière, F., Saribatur, Z. (eds.) Proceedings of the Fifth Workshop on Trends and Applications of Answer Set Programming (TAASP'22) (2022). http://www.kr.tuwien.ac.at/events/taasp22/papers/TAASP_2022_paper_5.pdf

17. Czarnecki, K., Helsen, S., Eisenecker, U.W.: Formalizing cardinality-based feature models and their specialization. Softw. Process: improv. pract. 10(1), 7–29 (2005). https://doi.org/10.1002/spip.213

18. Dhungana, D., Grünbacher, P., Rabiser, R.: The DOPLER meta-tool for decision-oriented variability modeling: a multiple case study. Autom. Softw. Eng. 18, 77–114 (2011). https://doi.org/10.1007/s10515-010-0076-6

19. Eiter, T., Faber, W., Fink, M., Woltran, S.: Complexity results for answer set programming with bounded predicate arities and implications. Ann. Math. Artif. Intell. 51(2–4), 123–165 (2007). https://doi.org/10.1007/S10472-008-9086-5

20. Erdem, E., Gelfond, M., Leone, N.: Applications of answer set programming. AI Mag. **37**(3), 53–68 (2016). https://doi.org/10.1609/aimag.v37i3.2678

21. Falkner, A.A., Friedrich, G., Haselböck, A., Schenner, G., Schreiner, H.: Twenty-five years of successful application of constraint technologies at Siemens. AI Mag. **37**(4), 67–80 (2016). https://doi.org/10.1609/AIMAG.V37I4.2688

22. Falkner, A.A., Friedrich, G., Schekotihin, K., Taupe, R., Teppan, E.C.: Industrial applications of answer set programming. Künstl. Intell. **32**(2–3), 165–176 (2018). https://doi.org/10.1007/s13218-018-0548-6

23. Falkner, A.A., Haselböck, A., Schenner, G., Schreiner, H.: Modeling and solving technical product configuration problems. Artif. Intell. Eng. Des. Anal. Manuf. **25**(2), 115–129 (2011). https://doi.org/10.1017/S0890060410000570

24. Falkner, A.A., Ryabokon, A., Schenner, G., Shchekotykhin, K.M.: OOASP: connecting object-oriented and logic programming. In: Calimeri, F., Ianni, G., Truszczynski, M. (eds.) Logic Programming and Nonmonotonic Reasoning - 13th International Conference, LPNMR 2015, Lexington, KY, USA, September 27–30, 2015. Proceedings, Lecture Notes in Computer Science, vol. 9345, pp. 332–345. Springer (2015). https://doi.org/10.1007/978-3-319-23264-5_28

25. Fasth, M.: Evolution of product configuration: a journey through SICS and RISE (2023). https://www.cpq.se/the-cpq-blog/evolution-of-product-configuration-a-journey-through-sics-and-rise

26. Felfernig, A., Falkner, A., Benavides, D.: Feature Models: AI-Driven Design, Analysis and Applications. SpringerBriefs in Computer Science. Springer International Publishing, Cham (2024). https://doi.org/10.1007/978-3-031-61874-1

27. Felfernig, A., Friedrich, G., Jannach, D., Stumptner, M., Zanker, M.: Configuration knowledge representations for semantic web applications. Artif. Intell. Eng. Des. Anal. Manuf. **17**(1), 31–50 (2003). https://doi.org/10.1017/S0890060403171041

28. Felfernig, A., Hotz, L., Bagley, C., Tiihonen, J. (eds.): Knowledge-Based Configuration: From Research to Business Cases, 1st edn. Morgan Kaufmann Publishers Inc., San Francisco, CA (2014). ISBN: 2415817X

29. Fichte, J.K., Berre, D.L., Hecher, M., Szeider, S.: The silent (r)evolution of SAT. Commun. ACM **66**, 64–72 (2023). https://doi.org/10.1145/3560469

30. Frühwirth, T.: Principles of Rule-Based Programming. BoD-Books on Demand (2025)

31. Garey, M.R., Johnson, D.S.: Computers and Intractability: A Guide to the Theory of NP-Completeness. W. H. Freeman and Company (1979)

32. Gebser, M., Kaminski, R., Kaufmann, B., Lindauer, M., Ostrowski, M., Romero, J., Schaub, T., Thiele, S., Wanko, P.: Potassco User Guide version 2.2.0 (2019). https://github.com/potassco/guide/releases/tag/v2.2.0

33. Gebser, M., Kaminski, R., Kaufmann, B., Romero, J., Schaub, T.: Progress in clasp series 3. In: Calimeri, F., Ianni, G., Truszczynski, M. (eds.) Logic Programming and Nonmonotonic Reasoning, Lecture Notes in Computer Science, vol. 9345, pp. 368–383. Springer (2015). https://doi.org/10.1007/978-3-319-23264-5_31

34. Gebser, M., Kaminski, R., Kaufmann, B., Schaub, T.: Answer Set Solving in Practice. Synthesis Lectures on Artificial Intelligence and Machine Learning, Morgan and Claypool Publishers (2012)

35. Gebser, M., Kaminski, R., Ostrowski, M., Schaub, T., Thiele, S.: On the input language of ASP grounder gringo. In: Erdem, E., Lin, F., Schaub, T. (eds.) Logic Programming and Nonmonotonic Reasoning, 10th International Conference, LPNMR 2009, Potsdam, Germany, September 14–18, 2009. Proceedings, Lecture Notes in Computer Science, vol. 5753, pp. 502–508. Springer, Berlin (2009). https://doi.org/10.1007/978-3-642-04238-6_49

36. Gelfond, M., Kahl, Y.: Knowledge Representation, Reasoning, and the Design of Intelligent Agents: The Answer-Set Programming Approach. Cambridge University Press, New York, NY, USA (2014)

37. Guns, T.: Increasing modeling language convenience with a universal n-dimensional array, CPPY as python-embedded example. In: Proceedings of the 18th Workshop on Constraint Modelling and Reformulation at CP (Modref 2019), vol. 19 (2019)

38. Haag, A.: "Dealing" with configurable products in the sap business suite. In: Jannach, D., Felfernig, A. (eds.) Papers from the Configuration Workshop at IJCAI'05, pp. 68–71 (2005)

39. Haag, A., Haag, L.: Further empowering variant tables for mass customization. Int. J. Ind. Eng. Manag. **10**(2), 155–170 (2019). https://doi.org/10.24867/IJIEM-2019-2-236

40. Hadzic, T., Subbarayan, S., Jensen, R., Andersen, H., Møller, J., Hulgaard, H.: Fast backtrack-free product configuration using a precompiled solution space representation. PETO (2009)

41. Hogan, A., Blomqvist, E., Cochez, M., D'amato, C., Melo, G.D., Gutierrez, C., Kirrane, S., Gayo, J.E.L., Navigli, R., Neumaier, S., Ngomo, A.C.N., Polleres, A., Rashid, S.M., Rula, A., Schmelzeisen, L., Sequeda, J., Staab, S., Zimmermann, A.: Knowledge graphs. ACM Comput. Surv. **54**(4) (2021). https://doi.org/10.1145/3447772

42. ISO: ISO/IEC 13211-1:1995 - Information technology - Programming languages - Prolog (1995). https://www.iso.org/standard/21413.html

43. Junker, U.: Configuration. In: Rossi et al. [57], pp. 837–873

44. Kang, K.C., Cohen, S.G., Hess, J.A., Novak, W.E., Peterson, A.S.: Feature-oriented domain analysis (FODA) feasibility study. Software Engineering Institute, Carnegie Mellon University, Technical report (1990)

45. Kowalski, R.A.: Algorithm = logic + control. Commun. ACM **22**(7), 424–436 (1979). https://doi.org/10.1145/359131.359136

46. Lewis, M., Radbill, D.: Gartner magic quadrant for configure, price and quote applications (2023). https://www.gartner.com/en/documents/5019831

47. Lifschitz, V.: Answer Set Programming. Springer, Berlin (2019). https://doi.org/10.1007/978-3-030-24658-7

48. McGuinness, D.L., Wright, J.R.: An industrial-strength description-logics-based configurator platform. IEEE Intell. Syst. **13**(4), 69–77 (1998). https://doi.org/10.1109/5254.708435

49. Mears, C., Schutt, A., Stuckey, P.J., Tack, G., Marriott, K., Wallace, M.: Modelling with option types in MiniZinc. In: Simonis, H. (ed.) Integration of AI and OR Techniques in Constraint Programming - 11th International Conference, CPAIOR 2014, Cork, Ireland, May 19–23, 2014. Proceedings, Lecture Notes in Computer Science, vol. 8451, pp. 88–103. Springer, Berlin (2014). https://doi.org/10.1007/978-3-319-07046-9_7

50. Mendonça, M., Branco, M., Cowan, D.D.: S.P.L.O.T.: software product lines online tools. In: Arora, S., Leavens, G.T. (eds.) Companion to the 24th Annual ACM SIGPLAN Conference on Object-Oriented Programming, Systems, Languages, and Applications, OOPSLA 2009, October 25–29, 2009, Orlando, Florida, USA, pp. 761–762. ACM (2009). https://doi.org/10.1145/1639950.1640002

51. Munoz, R.: The Forrester Wave$^{TM}$: Configure, Price, Quote Solutions, Q1 2025 (2025). https://www.forrester.com/report/RES181962

52. Myllärniemi, V., Tiihonen, J., Raatikainen, M., Felfernig, A.: Using answer set programming for feature model representation and configuration. In: ConfWS'14, pp. 1–8 (2014)

53. Narboni, G.A.: On rule systems whose consistency can be locally maintained. AI Commun. **26**(1), 67–77 (2013). https://doi.org/10.3233/AIC-2012-0546

54. Nethercote, N., Stuckey, P.J., Becket, R., Brand, S., Duck, G.J., Tack, G.: MiniZinc: Towards a standard CP modelling language. In: Bessiere, C. (ed.) Principles and Practice of Constraint Programming - CP 2007, 13th International Conference, CP 2007, Providence, RI, USA, September 23–27, 2007, Proceedings, Lecture Notes in Computer Science, vol. 4741, pp. 529–543. Springer, Berlin (2007). https://doi.org/10.1007/978-3-540-74970-7_38

55. Potassco: Course on answer set solving in practice (2024). https://teaching.potassco.org/

56. Prud'homme, C., Fages, J.: Choco-solver: A java library for constraint programming. J. Open Source Softw. **7**(78), 1–6 (2022). https://doi.org/10.21105/joss.04708

57. Rossi, F., van Beek, P., Walsh, T. (eds.): Handbook of Constraint Programming. Elsevier Science (2006). ISBN 9780080463803. LCCN 2006048518

58. Rühling, N., Schaub, T., Stolzmann, T.: Towards a formalization of configuration problems for ASP-based reasoning: preliminary report. In: ConfWS-2023: 25th International Configuration Workshop (2023), vol. 3509, pp. 85–94. CEUR (2023)

59. Rühling, N., Schaub, T., Wanko, P.: Formalizing ASP-based product configuration: work in progress. In: Proceedings of the Eighth Workshop on Trends and Applications of Answer Set Programming (TAASP'25) (2025). https://taasp.at/2025/assets/paper/1_Formalizing_ASP_based_Produc.pdf

60. Russell, S., Norvig, P.: Artificial Intelligence: A Modern Approach, 4th edn, Pearson (2020). http://aima.cs.berkeley.edu/

61. Sabharwal, A.: Modern SAT solvers: key advances and applications (2011). https://courses.cs.washington.edu/courses/csep573/11wi/lectures/ashish-satsolvers.pdf

62. Sabin, D., Weigel, R.: Product configuration frameworks - a survey. IEEE Intell. Syst. **13**(4), 42–49 (1998). https://doi.org/10.1109/5254.708432

63. Schenner, G., Taupe, R.: Encoding object-oriented models in MiniZinc. In: 15th International Workshop on Constraint Modelling and Reformulation (ModRef'16) (2016). http://cp2016.a4cp.org/program/workshops/ws-modref-papers/Taupe.pdf

64. Schulte, C., Tack, G.: View-based propagator derivation. Constr. Int. J. **18**(1), 75–107 (2013). https://doi.org/10.1007/S10601-012-9133-Z

65. Stuckey, P.J., Marriott, K., Tack, G.: The MiniZinc Handbook (2025). https://docs.minizinc.dev/

66. Stuckey, P.J., Tack, G.: Enumerated types and type extensions for MiniZinc. In: Schaus, P. (ed.) Integration of Constraint Programming, Artificial Intelligence, and Operations Research - 19th International Conference, CPAIOR 2022, Los Angeles, CA, USA, June 20–23, 2022, Proceedings, Lecture Notes in Computer Science, vol. 13292, pp. 374–389. Springer, Berlin (2022). https://doi.org/10.1007/978-3-031-08011-1_25

67. Tack, G., Comploi-Taupe, R., Falkner, A., Schenner, G.: MiniZinc with objects. Constraints (2025). https://doi.org/10.1007/s10601-025-09380-3

68. Theeg, G., Vlasenko, S. (eds.): Railway Signalling & Interlocking: International Compendium. Edition Eurailpress (2018)

69. Tiihonen, J., Anderson, A.: Varisales. In: Felfernig et al. [28], Chap. 26, pp. 309–318

70. Tiihonen, J., Korppila, V.V., Heimonen, J., Anderson, A.: Structure oriented sales configuration of precast concrete production factories. In: Proceedings of the 22nd International Configuration Workshop, pp. 1–8. Università degli Studi di Padova (2020). https://www.eventhelpr.com/files/events/RqdLM1Pt/attachments/proceedings-cws-2020_JEqWr6vY.pdf

**Open Access** This chapter is licensed under the terms of the Creative Commons Attribution-NonCommercial-NoDerivatives 4.0 International License (http://creativecommons.org/licenses/by-nc-nd/4.0/), which permits any noncommercial use, sharing, distribution and reproduction in any medium or format, as long as you give appropriate credit to the original author(s) and the source, provide a link to the Creative Commons license and indicate if you modified the licensed material. You do not have permission under this license to share adapted material derived from this chapter or parts of it.

The images or other third party material in this chapter are included in the chapter's Creative Commons license, unless indicated otherwise in a credit line to the material. If material is not included in the chapter's Creative Commons license and your intended use is not permitted by statutory regulation or exceeds the permitted use, you will need to obtain permission directly from the copyright holder.

# Chapter 6
# Quality

**Abstract** Successful configurators are based on high quality: User expectation (requirements), product offering (configurability), technical correctness (feasibility), and producibility must align. Quality affects all aspects of product configuration: Knowledge base (modeling), user interface, data sources, and configuration result. Error prevention (instead of only correction) leads to cost reduction. This chapter sheds light on typical problems related to quality, presents strategies to ensure high quality, drawing from good software development practices, and describes possible causes for configuration project failures.

Like any other piece of software, Product Configuration faces quality issues of various kinds, and will be successful only if the underlying problems can be solved and high quality is achieved. Several decades ago, elaborate quality measures and processes were developed and successfully applied to waterfall-style projects (e.g., by Barry Boehm [17]). They culminated in the 1980s in Total Quality Management (TQM) [6]. However, activities such as requirements and system specifications, code reviews, test plans, test protocols, risk evaluations, etc., consume significant human efforts and were questioned with the rising pressure for cost reduction and accelerating technology changes and demand for new functionalities. In 2001, the Agile Software Development approach [2] tried to improve this situation by focusing on customer collaboration, responding to change, and (continuously) working software. Unfortunately, some adopters see the agile approach as an opportunity to neglect quality management even more. This may be acceptable to a certain degree[1] for uncritical products and websites that survive only a few months. On the other hand, the digital revolution of the 2000s has triggered vast research and investments in the field of User Experience (UX), which places more emphasis on user needs and emotions when developing and testing software products [15].

---

[1] In practice, it is always necessary to find a reasonable balance between quality and cost.

© Siemens Aktiengesellschaft Österreich 2026

R. Comploi-Taupe and A. Falkner, *Product Configuration*,
SpringerBriefs in Computer Science,
https://doi.org/10.1007/978-3-032-17163-4_6

To achieve sufficient quality for larger and long-lived products, we must adhere to a more conservative approach: Agile principles backed by efficient quality assurance, including at least:

- an up-to-date specification of the user requirements,
- a system architecture reviewed by all stakeholders,
- easily understandable code (which makes comments almost unnecessary),
- a compact set of test cases that cover all user requirements and non-functional requirements (response times, memory usage, etc.) and as much of the code as possible,
- a precise definition of quality metrics that can be automatically measured,
- an automated build and deployment system that runs and checks all tests and metrics (and allows for nightly builds),
- a reliable version control system (configuration management system), and
- a motivated team, including a responsible person who confirms the go-live.

Recent advances in AI-based code generation [20] might help reduce human effort. However, extreme care must be taken to ensure that the product owner's full intent, and nothing else, is implemented.

## 6.1  Challenges for the Quality of Product Models

A primary source of problems is that the basic ingredients of the product model do not align sufficiently. Most importantly, each product model must meet customer requirements. Let us look at the example from Chap. 3 and Fig. 3.8, the configurable folding bike: Customers want bikes in various sizes and types, e.g., off-road, vegan, electric (roughly shown in Fig. 3.6). On the other hand, we have the set of all technically feasible products (as defined in Fig. 3.5). For example, technical feasibility means that the seatpost comes in defined lengths, that both wheels must have reflectors (or not), that an electric bike needs a motor and a battery, etc. Hopefully, the overlap between wishes and technical feasibility is not as small as depicted in the Venn diagram of Fig. 6.1. In addition, there are the configurator (which allows the user to select from the feasible products) and the production facility (in a very simple way expressed in Fig. 3.7). And again, some aspects may not overlap with the others.

All this leads to the following typical problems (see Fig. 6.1):

- First, we could have products that we can offer (meaning configure), but they are never ordered. For example, titanium frames because the customer group doesn't include ambitious sportspersons, just ordinary people. Maintaining those variants causes unnecessary effort and could be avoided by cleaning up our offering, e.g., with variability management [4, 10, 12, 16].
- If the configurator allows ordering products that make no sense at all, we have a more serious problem. For example, if electric bikes were configurable without a battery because we modeled the battery as optional instead of mandatory. Or

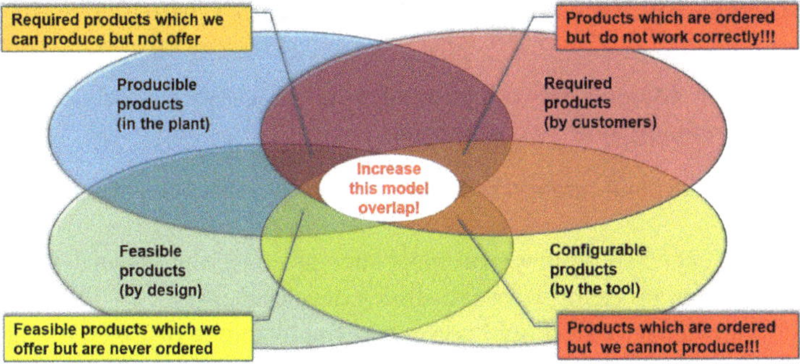


**Fig. 6.1** Challenges for the quality of product models (*Source* Own work)

reflectors on just one wheel because we forgot to add the corresponding constraint. Then customers will complain, we may need to pay back money, lose business, and even lose customers. Such mistakes must be avoided.

- If we add the production line to the equation, we can have products that make sense (i.e., are feasible) and could actually be produced, but we don't have them in our configurator. For example, a second (spare) battery. Or integrated front and back lights for electric bikes. Users would order them if we offered them, so we lose business.
- The worst case is that products are ordered and feasible, but we cannot produce them. Perhaps we ran out of telescope seatposts and cannot produce them any longer because of a broken machine. So we cannot serve orders from tall customers, which will make them angry, and we might face penalty costs or similar.

Therefore, it is vital to increase the small overlap of the figure as much as possible, e.g., with a single source of truth where all involved tools, like the configuration tool and production planning, and the product data build upon the same database (see Sect. 3.2). Or with state-of-the-art quality management [18], including peer reviews, automated regression testing [5, 11], etc.

Test-driven development [1] will help a lot: For each new or changed requirement or interface, we consider the effects on the existing solution (user interface, data interfaces, configuration results, production aspects) and define or change appropriate test cases before we do the corresponding coding. Thus, we reduce the chance that we overlook subtle interdependencies and that inconsistencies in the overlaps of Fig. 6.1 creep in. The necessary efforts will typically pay off in due time because the test cases can be reused a thousand times for automated regression testing of each major, minor, or batch deployment or nightly builds, which ensures that nothing was unintentionally broken. Without any further human effort (except briefly checking the summary of error messages when noticed by the automated process), this keeps the quality high and therefore avoids non-compliance costs and the risk of penalties.

## 6.2  Success Factors for Quality in Product Configuration

To achieve such comprehensive high quality, all processes, aspects, and levels of product configuration must be considered:

- The result of the configuration task must be correct, complete, and appropriate for the user.
  This can be achieved by powerful tools such as constraint solvers (see Chap. 5) and well-proven processes (like test-driven development).
- A good knowledge base should serve as a single source of truth. It must match the product design. There must not be contradictions or redundancies in it, and it must be maintainable.
  This can be supported by good analytic and debugging tools (e.g., FAMA [3] provides quality metrics for feature models; diagnosis algorithms help with the detection and diagnosis of modeling errors [7]) and backed by an efficient version control system (such as Git). Proper refactoring keeps the knowledge base clean and effective to use (in contrast to just piling one special case upon another).
- Typically, the knowledge is based on external data like product details, costs, prices, etc. That information must be well-integrated into the knowledge base; it must be accessible and feasible, and it must be kept up-to-date.
  Precise and maintained specifications of data interfaces and adherence to standards[2] facilitate these tasks.
- And last but not least, user interaction must be satisfactory. For a product to be useful, it must be both usable and utilitarian. Utility refers to the product's ability to fulfill its intended function and provide genuine value to users by solving real problems or meeting specific needs effectively. Usability, on the other hand, defines how easily, efficiently, and intuitively users can interact with the product to achieve their goals, encompassing factors like learnability, efficiency, memorability, error prevention, and overall user satisfaction with the interface and experience. In this context, usefulness is defined as the intersection of utility and usability [13].
  For usage to be efficient and intuitive, usability must be considered in product configuration. Usability studies and user testing can help avoid usability errors such as redundant input or inconsistent configurations. Usability workshops can help identify the main user classes, their most important workflows, and helpful widgets to support them. Ideally, the user is guided by an intelligent flow of questions and options that reflect the user's mental model of the product to be configured [14].
  Finally, a clear definition and compliance with company-specific UI guidelines lead to a unique and recognizable look-and-feel for the configurator.

All of this is known from classical software development: tools, databases, interfaces, usability, etc. Therefore, one needs good software engineering practices [18] to achieve high-quality product configuration. This leads to some costs, and we need to ensure that their benefits outweigh them: smoother processes, reduced errors, fewer

---

[2] At least to industry standards as set by important players such as SAP.

non-compliance costs, and penalties. It is well known [19] that the earlier an error is found in the product lifecycle, the smaller are the costs of correction.

Therefore, we must strive to avoid errors right from the start: Cost reduction through error prevention (instead of correction). A good start is a good design for the configurator, e.g., by applying the KISS principle (Keep It Simple, Stupid!) and a modular[3] approach (separation of concerns, divide and conquer)—see Chap. 7 for concrete ideas. The modeling language should be as high-level as possible, i.e., an executable specification: It directly represents the modeler's intent, without error-prone manual translations (coding in a lower-level language).

## 6.3  How Configurator Projects Can Fail

Despite the scientific bias to publish positive results, there is enough evidence [8–10] that not every configurator project is a success. Costs can easily run out of hand, as Fig. 6.2 sketches: Typically, development costs are high at the start of the project and flatten during the extension or maintenance phase. Income starts only later, after the configurator is deployed and used by customers. Whether it pays off depends on the sales volume in relation to the ongoing maintenance cost.

Configuration projects can fail in various phases. Haug et al. [9] outline an overall framework for understanding failure in configuration projects. Using this framework, eight failed configurator projects are investigated (for sales and/or engineering in various industries such as electronics, chemical process systems, and buildings—with product specification times ranging from several weeks to months). These cases demonstrate that poor decision-making in one phase can have escalating negative consequences in subsequent phases until the configurator project eventually fails. Figure 6.3, based upon their work, shows that failure as well as termination can occur in all phases of the project lifecycle. The cycle starts with defining the content (at the top of the figure), and a successful project runs through four more main phases (indicated by the green arrows in the figure). For each of these phases, another group of stakeholders carries the main responsibilities:

- Decision-makers, e.g., product management or line management, are responsible for project scoping; that is, they want a product configurator with certain functionality.
- Knowledge engineers are responsible for the configurator specification; that is, they formulate the product structure and variety.
- Developers implement the configurator based on the specification.

---

[3] This allows for easier integration of third-party software. However, care must be taken not to introduce inconsistencies, deficiencies, and masses of unnecessary but potentially risky code. In the long run, it is often better to code a small function oneself instead of using an arbitrary library that supplies (an approximation of) it among much more stuff.

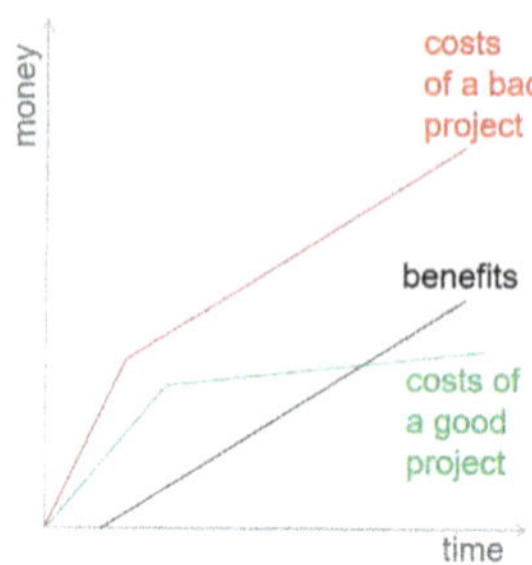


**Fig. 6.2**  Costs and benefits of configuration projects (*Source* Own work)

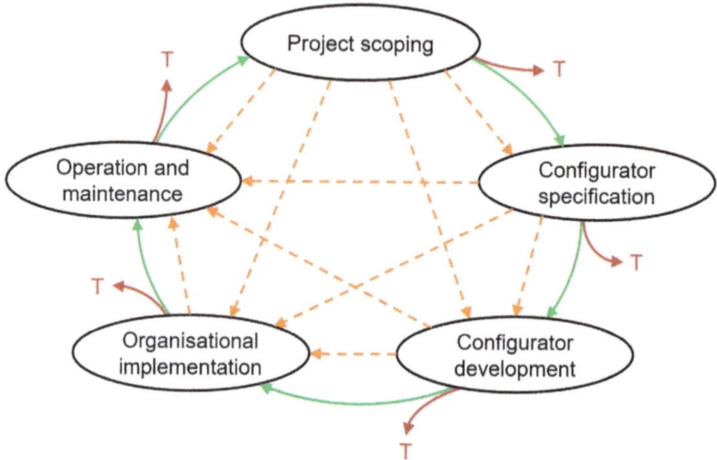


**Fig. 6.3**  Causes of configuration project failure (*Source* Own work, inspired by Fig. 2 in [9])

- Organizational implementers, e.g., the IT department, manage the deployment into the entire organization.
- Configurator users will provide (explicit or implicit) feedback during operations, which leads to maintenance and might start a new cycle for extensions and/or improvements.

Instead of continuing to the next phase, the configurator project may be terminated in any phase (indicated by the red arrows in Fig. 6.3). For example, already at project scoping, e.g., after the initial planning, it may turn out that the project will not be effective, or that the products are not suited for configuration at all (e.g., too complex, not modular enough, or insufficiently standardized).

Often, it turns out during development that it is more expensive than expected, or that the implementation is not possible at all with the available software stack. This means that the stakeholders are not content with what can be achieved with the tool, or the users are not satisfied. Therefore, they refuse to use the tool. In some cases, it was realized that developers and/or implementers could not manage the maintenance and the rapid change of the product efficiently enough.

Importantly, decisions or mistakes in early phases may have effects that later lead to failure (the orange arrows in Fig. 6.3 connect the phases with the failure causes to those phases where the project had to be terminated). This is especially painful when the entire cycle is completed and failure occurs only at the end, as indicated by the arrow from "Project scoping" to "Operation and maintenance" in the figure. For example, decision-makers demanded a product that was so complex that it could not be configured by the users after being specified, developed, and deployed. Or they did not consider maintenance, which led to unusability after a few months of use. In such a case, when a project has to be stopped so late, a lot of invested money is lost. For detailed information on the causes of failure, we refer to Haug et al. [9].

## Exercises

**Exercise 6.1** Figure 6.4 shows a sketch of a customer order[4] for 11 switches to control the sunblinds of eight windows (W1–W8).

- One simple switch for each window[5]: W1–W8
- A group switch for windows 1–4: W1234
- A group switch for windows 5–7: W567
- A central switch for all windows: W12345678

The following components are available from the supplier:

- Simple switch for exactly one window: S1W
- Group switch for up to 4 windows: S4W
- Group switch for up to 3 windows or groups: S3GW

Answer the following questions: Can the customer order be fulfilled by the supplier? How many pieces of each component type are needed?

**Exercise 6.2** Following up from Exercise 6.1: During preparation of fulfillment, we realize that our supplier no longer offers S3GW components, but instead a new component: S3G (group switch for up to three groups).

Can we still fulfill the customer order? What can we do? List the required components.

This really happened some years ago in a new home. The vendor had accepted the order three months earlier.

---

[4] Based on a real-life experience.

[5] Each window needs a simple switch that controls only that window for technical reasons.

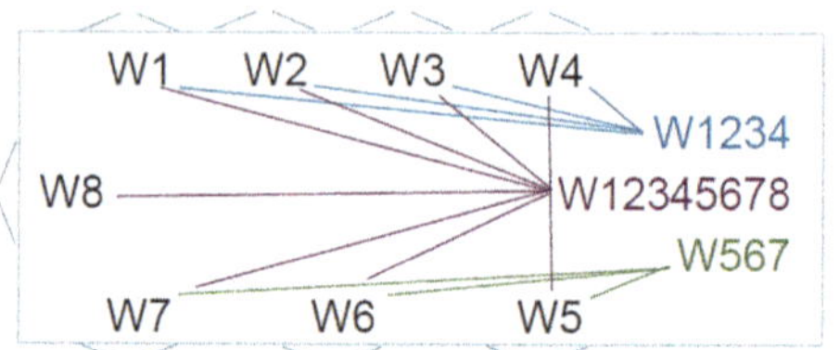


**Fig. 6.4** A sketch for control switches for sunblinds for eight windows (*Source* Own work)

**Exercise 6.3** Define a set of test cases for each of your solutions (models) for exercises from previous chapters. Each test case consists of input data and reference (output) data. Define both positive (i.e., valid solution) and negative (i.e., not leading to a valid solution) test cases. Aim for high coverage with a minimal number of test cases. Will you find flaws in your models?

## References


1. Beck, K.: Test-Driven Development: By Example. Addison-Wesley (2003)
2. Beck, K., Beedle, M., van Bennekum, A., Cockburn, A., Cunningham, W., Fowler, M., Grenning, J., Highsmith, J., Hunt, A., Jeffries, R., Kern, J., Marick, B., Martin, R.C., Mellor, S., Schwaber, K., Sutherland, J., Thomas, D.: Manifesto for agile software development (2021). https://agilemanifesto.org
3. Benavides, D., Segura, S., Trinidad, P., Cortés, A.R.: FAMA: tooling a framework for the automated analysis of feature models. In: Pohl, K., Heymans, P., Kang, K.C., Metzger, A. (eds.) First International Workshop on Variability Modelling of Software-Intensive Systems, VaMoS 2007, Limerick, Ireland, January 16–18, 2007. Proceedings, Lero Technical Report, vol. 2007–01, pp. 129–134 (2007). http://www.vamos-workshop.net/proceedings/VaMoS_2007_Proceedings.pdf
4. Blecker, T., Abdelkafi, N.: Complexity and variety in mass customization systems: analysis and recommendations. Manag. Decis. **44** (2006). https://doi.org/10.1108/00251740610680596
5. Falkner, A.A., Schenner, G., Friedrich, G., Ryabokon, A.: Testing object-oriented configurators with ASP. In: Mayer, W., Albert, P. (eds.) Proceedings of the Workshop on Configuration at ECAI 2012, Montpellier, France, August 27, 2012, CEUR Workshop Proceedings, vol. 958, pp. 21–26. CEUR-WS.org (2012). https://ceur-ws.org/Vol-958/paper4.pdf
6. Feigenbaum, A.V.: Total Quality Control. McGraw-Hill, New York (1983)
7. Felfernig, A., Schubert, M., Zehentner, C.: An efficient diagnosis algorithm for inconsistent constraint sets. Artif. Intell. Eng. Des. Anal. Manuf. **26**(1), 53–62 (2012). https://doi.org/10.1017/S0890060411000011
8. Haug, A., Hvam, L., Mortensen, N.H.: Definition and evaluation of product configurator development strategies. Comput. Ind. **63**(5), 471–481 (2012). https://doi.org/10.1016/J.COMPIND.2012.02.001
9. Haug, A., Shafiee, S., Hvam, L.: The causes of product configuration project failure. Comput. Ind. **108**, 121–131 (2019). https://doi.org/10.1016/J.COMPIND.2019.03.002
10. Haug, A., Shafiee, S., Hvam, L.: The costs and benefits of product configuration projects in engineer-to-order companies. Comput. Ind. **105**, 133–142 (2019). https://doi.org/10.1016/J.COMPIND.2018.11.005

11. Herud, K., Baumeister, J.: Testing product configuration knowledge bases declaratively. In: Reuss, P., Eisenstadt, V., Schönborn, J.M., Schäfer, J. (eds.) Proceedings of the LWDA 2022 Workshops: FGWM, FGKD, and FGDB, Hildesheim (Germany), Oktober 5–7th, 2022, CEUR Workshop Proceedings, vol. 3341, pp. 173–186. CEUR-WS.org (2022). https://ceur-ws.org/Vol-3341/WM-LWDA_2022_CRC_4316.pdf

12. Meinicke, J., Thüm, T., Schröter, R., Benduhn, F., Leich, T., Saake, G.: Mastering Software Variability with FeatureIDE. Springer, Berlin (2017). https://doi.org/10.1007/978-3-319-61443-4

13. Nielsen, J.: Usability 101: introduction to usability (2012). https://www.nngroup.com/articles/usability-101-introduction-to-usability/

14. Norman, D.: The Design of Everyday Things: Revised and Expanded Edition. Basic Books (2013)

15. Norman, D.A.: Why We Love (or Hate) Everyday Things. Perseus Books Group (2004)

16. Raben, C.H.: A product rationalization project part of a portfolio optimization program (2018). http://wiki.doing-projects.org/index.php/A_product_rationalization_project_part_of_a_portfolio_optimization_program

17. Selby, R.: Software Engineering: Barry W. Boehm's Lifetime Contributions to Software Development, Management, and Research. Practitioners. Wiley (2007)

18. Sommerville, I.: Software Engineering, 10th edn. Pearson Higher Ed (2016)

19. Stecklein, J.M., Dabney, J., Dick, B., Haskins, B., Lovell, R., Moroney, G.: Error cost escalation through the project life cycle. Technical report, National Aeronautics and Space Administration (NASA) (2004). https://ntrs.nasa.gov/citations/20100036670

20. Xu, F.F., Alon, U., Neubig, G., Hellendoorn, V.J.: A systematic evaluation of large language models of code. In: Chaudhuri, S., Sutton, C. (eds.) MAPS@PLDI 2022: 6th ACM SIGPLAN International Symposium on Machine Programming, San Diego, CA, USA, 13 June 2022, pp. 1–10. ACM (2022). https://doi.org/10.1145/3520312.3534862

**Open Access** This chapter is licensed under the terms of the Creative Commons Attribution-NonCommercial-NoDerivatives 4.0 International License (http://creativecommons.org/licenses/by-nc-nd/4.0/), which permits any noncommercial use, sharing, distribution and reproduction in any medium or format, as long as you give appropriate credit to the original author(s) and the source, provide a link to the Creative Commons license and indicate if you modified the licensed material. You do not have permission under this license to share adapted material derived from this chapter or parts of it.

The images or other third party material in this chapter are included in the chapter's Creative Commons license, unless indicated otherwise in a credit line to the material. If material is not included in the chapter's Creative Commons license and your intended use is not permitted by statutory regulation or exceeds the permitted use, you will need to obtain permission directly from the copyright holder.

# Chapter 7
# Performance Tuning

**Abstract** Finding an (optimal) solution to a configuration problem has exponential complexity in the worst case. Nevertheless, most practical cases can be solved sufficiently fast using techniques such as divide-and-conquer (workflows, decomposition), complexity reductions (relaxations), symmetry breaking, heuristics, and solver parametrization. In this chapter, we illustrate the exponential complexity of configuration problems to motivate the need for performance tuning, present some ideas to judge the relevant aspects of complexity, and explain in detail some important techniques to improve solving performance.

In Chap. 4 we have shown how product families can be specified in a tool-independent way, and in Chap. 5 we have introduced some technologies and tools to implement configurators for such specifications. In theory, this looks simple and straightforward. But in practice, we have to expect performance challenges due to the inherent complexity of the problem. A configuration problem (e.g., represented by a Feature Model as in Sect. 5.2) can be mapped to a SAT problem (see Sect. 5.4) and SAT solving is NP-complete [16], which means exponential efforts in the worst case.

## 7.1 Motivating Example

Let us look at the consequences based on the following example of a product configuration task (similar to Figs. 5.2 and 4.4):

- $N$ hardware modules of 6 different types shall be placed in at most $N/10$ racks.
- Each rack can be filled horizontally with up to 20 modules.
- Each module has 3 Boolean parameters.

How many different configurations are possible? We use combinatorics to calculate the numbers step by step, starting from the basic values such as the domain sizes of properties. For independent parts, we multiply the variant numbers. For alternatives, we add the numbers:

- For a module, the first Boolean parameter gives us two options (T,F). With the second, we have $2 \times 2 = 4$ combinations (TT, TF, FT, FF). With the third, we

© Siemens Aktiengesellschaft Österreich 2026

R. Comploi-Taupe and A. Falkner, *Product Configuration*,

SpringerBriefs in Computer Science,

https://doi.org/10.1007/978-3-032-17163-4_7

reach $2 \times 2 \times 2 = 8$ combinations (TTT, TTF, TFT, TFF, FTT, FTF, FFT, FFF). If all parameters have the same range (as here 2), we can express it more concisely with an exponent: $numberOfValues^{numberOfParameters}$, i.e., $2^3$.

- As modules come with 6 possible types, we get in total $6 \times 8 = 48$ different module configurations.
- In how many ways can we place them in the 20 slots of a rack? Just taking the slot number as an additional property with 20 values (and thus multiplying 48 with 20) is not correct because it can assign each of the 48 module configurations only one slot number. However, the same module configuration can be assigned to different slots in a rack. Therefore, we must consider the module configurations as potential values for 20 slot variables for each rack.
- As the product specification (see above) bounds the number of racks to $N/10$, we have at most $20 \times N/10 = 2 \times N$ slots for the $N$ modules. The binomial coefficient

$$\binom{2 \times N}{N}$$

  represents the number of ways to distribute $N$ items over $2 \times N$ positions and can be approximated with the Stirling formula $2^{2 \times N}/\sqrt{\pi \times N}$.
- Now we can combine (i.e., multiply) everything: $N$ modules (with 48 variants each) have together $48^N$ possible configurations. For the number of assignment variants (possible placements in $N/10$ racks), we just take the much more influential numerator of the Stirling approximation above: $2^{2 \times N} = 4^N$.
- The total (unconstrained) search space is approximately $48^N \times 4^N = 192^N$, i.e., exponential in $N$ with a large base.

Typically, constraints (e.g., certain module types have some fixed parameter values, certain parameter settings require or exclude some module positions, etc.) will reduce the solution space (i.e., the feasible configurations) to a tiny fraction of the search space which is computationally expensive to find.

Therefore, we can assume that the size of the search space somehow reflects how long we need to find a solution, e.g., a millisecond for checking a million of configuration variants. This means that in our example, troubles begin at a size of a billion. Figure 7.1 shows that it runs out of hand even for a very small number of modules, i.e., $N = 4$. Often, only a combination of tuning approaches helps. In the example, we apply some approaches which will be explained in more detail further down in this section.

*Divide and conquer*: If we can assign modules of different types independently to separate racks (i.e., we do not mix module types in a rack), we split up the large problem (assigning $N$ modules of any type to up to $N/10$ frames) to 6 smaller problems (each for assigning fewer modules of the same type to fewer frames). To make the calculation easier, we assume an equal distribution of types (i.e., a sixth of the modules for each type). The modules come now only in $2^3 = 8$ variants (as the type is fixed) which leads to the following approximation of the search space size for each type: $8^{N/6} \times 4^{N/6}$—compare with the formula above. For approximating the

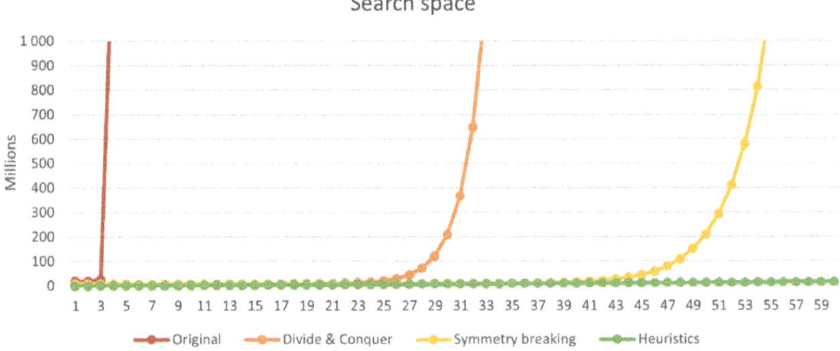

Fig. 7.1  Search space size for different tuning approaches (x axis: number of modules; y axis: search space size) (*Source* Own work)

solving time, we need not multiply the possibilities of the 6 types, but just add them up because solving for the 6 types runs independently, even in parallel—hence the factor (not exponent) of 6 in the total number: $6 \times 32^{N/6}$. The reduction of the base allows us to configure ca. 30 modules, which is still far below the capacity of only 2 racks.

*Symmetry breaking*: If the position of modules is not important, we can fill the racks from left to right (in addition to divide-and-conquer), i.e., we enforce one of the many symmetrical (equally useful) solutions. This leaves only the numbers for the different module configurations and the total size of the (computational) search space is $6 \times 8^{N/6}$. Despite the performance boost, more than 60 modules (3 racks) are still out of reach.

*Heuristics*: They often find a solution in (nearly) linear time. In our example, this could, e.g., be based on exploiting a statistical relationship between position and parameter settings of a module. Huge problems (if they are not too complicated) can be solved reliably only by such an approach. Heuristic search includes approaches such as iterative repair, simulated annealing, genetic algorithms, and ant colony optimization [8].

## 7.2  Measuring and Tackling Complexity

The preceding example shows that seemingly simple problems can get complex when it comes to solutions. So far, we have dealt with the notion of computational complexity [9, 29]. For a comprehensive view, however, we also need to consider system complexity [28]. In the field of product configuration, we can ignore the dynamic aspect of communicating agents, but we have (potentially many thousands of) components and features which are linked to a certain degree via constraints. Often, those dependencies are not completely defined. The complexity depends on

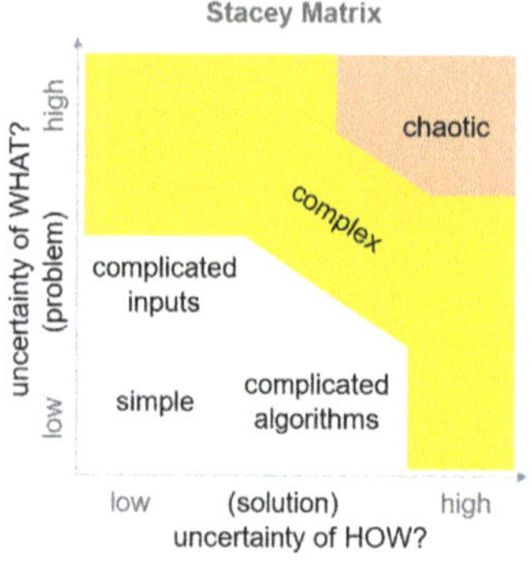


|              | Problem (WHAT?)                    | Solution (HOW?)        |
|--------------|------------------------------------|------------------------|
| **Domain**      | Product line specification         | Configurator (tool)    |
| **Application** | Individual product requirements    | Configuration result   |

**Fig. 7.2** What and how—-problem and solution (*Source* Own work)

the uncertainties of both the problem and the solution. Figure 7.2 gives an overview of different degrees of complexity and can serve the selection of proper tools for the different situations [32]:

- Simple = easily knowable
- Complicated = not simple, but still knowable
- Complex = not fully knowable, but reasonably predictable
- Chaotic = neither knowable nor predictable.

Simple and even complicated problems are addressable with state-of-the-art representations and tools, such as listed in Chap. 5. Complex problems involve many unknowns and unforeseeable dependencies, so that special attention is necessary to tackle them. The only way to deal with chaotic problems is to try to improve certainty in both dimensions: requirements elicitation and evaluation of technology and algorithms.

In practice, we can define *configuration complexity = size × complicatedness × uncertainty*. This affects both domain modeling (product line specification) and application (configuration of an individual product)—see the right-hand side of Fig. 7.2.

- Size is important for modeling because large models quickly become incomprehensible and difficult to maintain. Furthermore, analytics such as checking the model consistency gets more expensive. Also solving depends strongly on the size. Due to its potentially exponential nature, a small increase can lead to intractability (see the example above where 54 modules can be managed with symmetry breaking, but 55 cannot). Even if some algorithms have only low-polynomial (e.g., quadratic) runtime behaviour, sufficiently large inputs can cause unacceptably long answering times.
- Complicatedness, on the other hand, is defined by the number of the constraints and their size and structure. Complicated systems have many constraints and many dependencies [7], and even for medium-sized systems it is not easy to compute all compliant solutions by hand or by programming. Solving techniques such as

those discussed in Chap. 5 can handle this, but their performance depends on the constrainedness of the problem: For under-constrained[1] problems it is comparably easy to find a solution, and for over-constrained problems there are strategies to find proofs for inconsistency (nogoods, unsatisfiable cores) fast. We could use a problem's constraint-variable-ratio (e.g., sum of sizes of all constraints divided by the number of all variables) as an indication for complexity, but would still need to evaluate at which values performance of which tools starts to degrade.[2]

- Uncertainty in modeling often comes from the ambiguity or imprecision of product descriptions in natural language. Product experts tend to omit facts which are completely clear and self-evident to them. The process of implementing the product line specification in a tool depends on the expressiveness and power of its modeling language. We hypothesize that the easier understandable the modeling language, the smaller is the perceived complexity of the problem description.

It would be good to have a metric to control complexity, e.g., clearly defined and easily computable values for size, complicatedness, and uncertainty. Then we could calculate a total value for each product specification and use it to estimate the efforts to implement a configurator and the expected performance of its solver. Repeating this for each version would help to keep track of where complexity of the problem (and thus solving performance) starts to run out of hand, and to predict the costs for maintaining the model. If we want to see more details, we could even show all three values (not just their product) in a radar chart [30]: the total number of decision variables, the total size of all constraints, the confidence in the correctness and completeness of the model. We could even add additional properties such as the power of the solver. Unfortunately, this is not simple: We need some canonical representation of the problem and some proof that the calculated numbers are significant for the predictions. The latter can be achieved by a well-chosen set of regression tests with a good case coverage and documenting their runtimes in relation to the corresponding values of the metrics. A canonical representation for a subset of (comparably simple) configuration problems could be compressed variant tables (cf. Fig. 5.1), and their c-complexity[3] be a single indicator for both size and constrainedness.

Above we have defined $complexity = size \times complicatedness \times uncertainty$. How to tackle it?

1. Uncertain? Formalize! Chap. 4 introduced a formal representation for product lines, comprising product structure, component types and properties, cross-tree dependencies, and incompatibilities. It is important to translate all natural-

---

[1] Basically, an underconstrained problem is one that has many solutions, and an overconstrained problem is one that has very few or even no solutions [25].

[2] Satisfiability theory [17] knows that clause-variable-ratio (number of all clauses divided by number all variables) is a good indicator for the hardness of solving randomly generated problems with a value around 4 for the hardest problems (i.e., where solving took longest in average). Unfortunately, we do not know whether this holds for industrial instances and in general for constraint problems, although we could expect it because similar solving strategies are used for SAT solvers and constraint solvers.

[3] The sum of all symbols in all c-tuples which represent unconstrained sub-products [15].

language descriptions of the product variety into such a clear and unambiguous model and use it as a single source of truth for all product knowledge. This will reduce misunderstandings, facilitate maintenance, and lower costs.

2. Too much? Reduce variety!
Variability management[4] is about methods to clean up the product offering and adjust it to the market needs. In order to achieve a good solver performance, the number of instances (selected components) must be kept small, e.g., by creating them on demand only. This helps to keep response time low and thus usability and user satisfaction high.

3. Too complicated? Remove special cases!
Basically, this is a task of product design, e.g., by embracing modularization and standardization. Proper modeling can help, by formulating rules and constraints in the simplest way. The principles of Agile Software Development [2] apply also here, e.g., the developers' mantra attributed to Kent Beck [18]: "Make it work, make it right, make it fast." That means to concentrate first on the most important product variants which quickly bring benefits to the customers. Ensure that the solution is correct and evaluate which extensions (with further variants) make sense. Only when the model is stable and performance is too weak, tuning shall be considered.

## 7.3 The Main Tuning Steps

To improve performance, one may consider the following steps in the given order:

1. **Reduce the variety**: This will have the highest effect because it affects all phases of the configuration lifecycle. Practically, it is a task of variability management, which is not really in the responsibility of knowledge engineers but in the responsibility of sales and product management. However, knowledge engineers can support standardization and modularization intensely, e.g., help to structure the model, to find commonalities, to reuse components, etc. Reducing the complexity of the configurable product can be guided by metrics as discussed above. As a rule of thumb, fewer features and/or fewer constraints lead to more efficiency, both in modeling and in solving.[5] Fewer features need not necessarily mean less variety or less business due to reduction of the offering. One can still offer special cases with help of other tools (e.g., extensions of the BOM to add tailor-made components), or keep offering and designing them manually and support only the main variants (that are easily customizable and configurable) with straightforward tooling so that an excellent configurator can increase sales of those variants.

2. **Select an expressive modeling language**: A powerful and easily understandable language such as introduced in Chap. 4 makes the specification of a product

---

[4] See Sect. 1.1 for a list of references on the topic of variability management.

[5] However, in solving, redundant constraints can sometimes improve performance.

family more efficient and maintainable. It may not remove the complexity of the product, but at least the complexity of its representation. Even if the configuration tool is already decided, such a high-level specification may be used and—in the best case automatically—translated to the proprietary representation. On the other hand, most commercial configurators have user-friendly modeling environments (knowledge editors, studios) with the advantage of good integration and the disadvantage of vendor lock-in.

3. **Tune the model**: This is definitely the main responsibility of knowledge engineers and where they can contribute most to good performance. Depending on the used techniques, the effect varies from moderate to very high. In the following, we describe some techniques in more details: Decomposition (including effective workflow and high-level configuration vs. low-level configuration), symmetry breaking, global constraints, and relaxation.

4. **Select a fitting solver**: In many cases, this is already decided, depending on history or company conventions. If not so, one should evaluate the options. There are several solver technologies with different strengths (see Chap. 5) and meanwhile also many vendors of commercial tools. For an overview, check the latest evaluations of consulting companies (e.g., Gartner's Magic Quadrant for Configure, Price and Quote Applications [21]) or solving contests (e.g., MiniZinc challenge, SAT competition). As there is no silver bullet, a proof-of-concept (POC) can help to find the best fitting tool, e.g., by listing the required concepts and check which tools fulfill them in the needed quality (see Fig. 7.3 for a sketch).

5. **Tune the solver parameters**: Many solvers offer lots of call parameters which can be set or changed to influence performance. These are settings about search strategies, multithreading, timeouts, default heuristics, and many more. Permanent testing and evaluation is necessary to achieve good results. Find some more details in Sect. 7.8.

6. **Improve operations**: Not only development, but also operations can have significant effect. In the era of DevOps, IT infrastructure and processes play an important role, e.g., intelligent caching can tremendously reduce the time needed for loading the rules from the knowledge base and the instances from a database or from files.

## 7.4 Decomposition

Breaking down a large problem into several independent (or only loosely coupled) sub-problems has a huge performance effect because it reduces the search space tremendously [25]. The example in Fig. 7.4 shows that it tackles directly the inherent exponential growth: Given a railway plan with 15 track segments, let us assume that each of them has a feature ($v1, \ldots, v15$) which can take one of ten values ($1, \ldots, 10$). This leads to a search space of $10^{15}$. The number of valid solutions is much

92



| **Concepts**: Typical **patterns** for product line specification | needed? | **Representations**: Different implementations in 100s of **tools** and languages - partly incomplete, partly very special, partly incompatible | | | | | | |
| --- | --- | --- | --- | --- | --- | --- | --- | --- |
| | | Vendor1 | Vendor2 | Vendor3 | ... | MiniZinc | Feature Models | ... |
| Components (materials) | yes | ✓ | ✓ | ✓ | | ✓ | ? | |
| Part-structure (is-part-of) | yes | ✓ | ? | ✓ | | ? | ✓ | |
| Type-hierarchy (is-kind-of) | yes | ✗ | ✗ | ✗ | | ✓ | ✗ | |
| Features (properties) | yes | ✓ | ✓ | ✓ | | ✓ | ✓ | |
| Relations (object links) | no | ✗ | ✓ | ✗ | | ✓ | ✗ | |
| Constraint tables | yes | ✓ | ✓ | ? | | ? | ✗ | |
| Number arithmetic | no | ✗ | ? | ✓ | | ✓ | ✗ | |
| Variants (typicals) | yes | ✓ | ✓ | ? | | ✗ | ✗ | |
| Subsystems (collaboration) | no | ? | ? | ✓ | | ✗ | ✗ | |
| Optimization (multi-goal) | yes | ? | ✗ | ✗ | | ✓ | ✗ | |
| ... many more | | | | | | | | |

**Fig. 7.3** There are many vendor-specific and open-source representations for the configuration concepts (*Source* Own work)

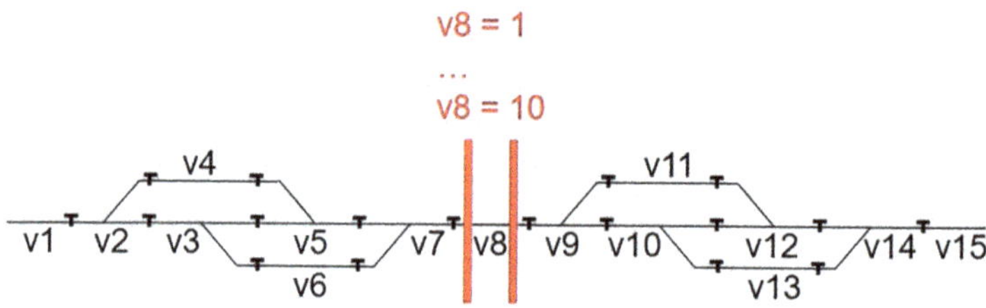


**Fig. 7.4** Separating a loosely coupled problem to improve performance (*Source* Own work)

smaller because there are several constraints between neighboring segments, which we do not need to know explicitly for this example. Unfortunately, we do not have independent sub-problems, but we can create 10 variants of the problem by fixing the value of segment v8. Then we can cut the variants at v8 into two parts. Solved independently, each of them has a search space of $10^7$. In total we get a search space of $10 \times 2 \times 10^7 = 2 \times 10^8$ which is exponentially less than originally.[6] If we could divide further into smaller parts then the reduction in search space and solver runtime would be even much higher.

Another idea is to separate features which the customer can select from those which can be automatically derived or defined later during order fulfillment. This leads to a comparably small sales configurator (with a reduced number of features and constraints) which efficiently helps the end customers configure their products. And in order to create the complete plan for manufacturing, it uses deterministic rules which are much faster than constraint solving because they do not need an elaborate search but just execution. SAP called this approach BOM explosion [3] because it means that only 10%, 5%, or even less than 1% of the complete bill of materials is

---

[6] Of course, this lower number does not mean that the total number of potential solutions is also smaller. We just reduce the work of the solver but letting it search in two half-sized problems so that we can add up the efforts instead of multiplying as for the number of solutions.

specified directly in the sales configurator and the huge rest is quickly (explosively) derived deterministically from those decisions.

Going one step further, one can separate the complete configuration task into several steps and thus define a structured workflow of comparably small subtasks. The drawback is reduced flexibility for the customer journey and perhaps weak user satisfaction. However, many—especially inexperienced or less knowledgeable—users prefer to be guided in such a way. Especially, if it is possible to let the user first set highly selective variables and to exploit deterministic rules or domain-specific heuristics in some of the steps [5, 6], then exponential growth of runtime may be reduced or avoided.

If users are expected to set many features in a short time (so that solving is permanently triggered and automatically set values continuously overwritten) then the UI may be changed so that it defers constraint solving to a user's "ready" signal. This means returning to an old-style mask-driven user interface which lets the user take several decisions and only start the solver on demand, e.g., when the user clicks a "continue" button. If there are constraints between the fields in a mask, this may allow the user to select inconsistent values, leading to unsatisfiability. To mitigate, a good solver is needed which helps the user by explaining the sources of the inconsistency.

## 7.5  Symmetry Breaking

A (seemingly) paradoxical way to improve performance is not to remove constraints, but to add constraints. If they are defined properly, they reduce or remove symmetrical solutions, i.e., solutions which differ only by irrelevant detail [4].

For example, assume that we have four hardware modules (A, B, C, D) and we must put them into four slots (1, 2, 3, 4). The number of possible solutions is $4! = 4 \times 3 \times 2 \times 1 = 24$. However, if it does not matter which module is put into which slot then all those solutions are equivalent (symmetric) and we can define one canonical solution, e.g., modules placed in lexicographic order.[7] This can be achieved by an additional constraint which enforces this unique solution, e.g., for any two modules, the module with the higher letter must be in a slot with a higher number. In this case (and of course even more for higher numbers of modules and slots) the constraint has a tremendous effect because it also does away with exponential growth in that context.

Unfortunately, this may not work in general for all kinds and combinations of symmetry-breaking constraints because each added constraint will add additional solving effort and the additional effort may be higher than the benefit of symmetry breaking. Therefore, this approach needs to be tested and evaluated thoroughly. But it is always worth a try, and especially permutational symmetry such as in the example

---

[7] A similar approach was shown in the example at the start of this chapter—together with an estimation of the resulting performance gains.

above is a promising candidate for performance improvements through symmetry-breaking constraints.


## 7.6   Special Constraints and Heuristics

Many solvers provide global constraints, i.e., constraints which affect many variables [24, 26]. Examples are all-equal (i.e., all variables in the constraint must have the same value), all-different (i.e., all variables in the constraint must have different values), and resource constraints (e.g., the sum of all values of one part of the variables must be greater than the sum of the other part). We recommend their usage because they are typically very efficient.

For common application areas such as packing problems or scheduling, there are special constraints such as spatial or temporal constraints (e.g., no overlaps) [26]. They make it easier to formulate the problem specification and have optimized implementations so that solving time is reduced.

So-called *streamlining constraints* are another approach to improve solving performance by adding constraints that partition the solution space to direct the search towards a small and structured part of the full combinatorial space [12].

Often, solvers use domain-independent, general heuristics to find a solution faster [8, 25, 27]. Some solvers give the possibility to specify problem-specific heuristics (or *search strategies*) [6, 10, 26]. Thus, one can take advantage of one's domain knowledge and code a special heuristic which helps the solver quickly find a solution to a special set of problems. For example, we may know that a special hardware configuration problem will be solved more easily if modules of a certain type are placed starting from the left while the other modules are placed starting from the right.


## 7.7   Relaxation

For some problems it might be possible to find a weaker, less constrained version of the problem, which can be solved very fast. For example, module placements in hardware configuration problems such as in the example in the beginning of this chapter can often (if some extra-ordinary constraints are ignored) be mapped to a bin-packing problem [19] for which efficient approximation algorithms exist. If some of the ignored constraints are indeed violated, e.g., by placing a certain module next to an incompatible other one, they must be resolved in a second step, e.g., by moving the incompatible module to another rack. This approach relies on the willingness of the user to accept also near-optimal solutions (as full optimality is mostly lost in the second step) and that the second step can resolve the inconsistencies fast.

In general, a relaxed version can be achieved by removing (or adapting) complicated, time-consuming constraints. Then very efficient techniques other than standard constraint solving may be used, e.g., if only linear constraints remain, we can solve the problem with (integer) linear programming. Of course, this results in too many potential solutions which need to be checked with the full product model to achieve the real valid solutions—either by filtering out the spurious (wrong) solutions or by using them as a starting point to get to the nearest real solution in some way.[8]

## 7.8  Solver Tuning

While in the previous sections a knowledge engineer had to write constraints or do other modeling we will give here a very brief overview about another possibility of performance tuning.

State-of-the-art solvers use various techniques to reduce runtime, e.g., backjumping (instead of simple backtracking) [25], unsatisfiable core extraction [1], conflict or no-good learning [11, 22], informed search strategies such as A* [25] or branch-and-bound algorithms [20], solver restarts [14], etc. They have default settings what techniques to use when. But they also have parameters which allow to change the settings, and if model tuning did not lead to satisfying results, one should try to play with those parameters. Different solvers have different parameters, e.g., for search strategies, timeouts, heuristics, etc.[9]

Unfortunately, there is no one single parameter setting, neither one simple heuristic nor one specific strategy, that will work for all problems [31]. And even if some strategy works well with a set of test cases, it might not work so well with another set of test cases. Therefore, permanent testing or regression testing and continuous evaluation is required to ensure that the parameter settings are still OK after changes to the model.

Modern solvers also offer support to automate this to a certain degree: Portfolio solvers [13] run different parameter settings in parallel or in sequence and proceed with the most promising one to find a solution fast. Thus, they can automatically tune their parameter settings for a given set of test cases. Similarly, parallel execution of different solver instances or different solvers can also improve the overall runtime if one of the solvers is faster than the others, e.g., because its chosen strategy is more successful than the others.

Another group of parameters comprises the number of restarts, the time until restart, and the distance of the restart position (large neighbourhood search [23], Monte Carlo tree search, etc.). Restart means if the solver doesn't find a solution

---

[8] This is similar to what linear programming solvers do to find a solution to a mixed integer problem or a linear integer problem: Find the best real number solution fast with linear solving and then search in its vicinity for integer solutions. In mixed integer programming, some solvers supply plug-ins which can handle even some non-linear constraints.

[9] For a concrete example, see the section on search annotations in the MiniZinc Handbook [26] or search for "strateg" there.

**Fig. 7.5** A variant of the tiling problem (*Source* Own work)

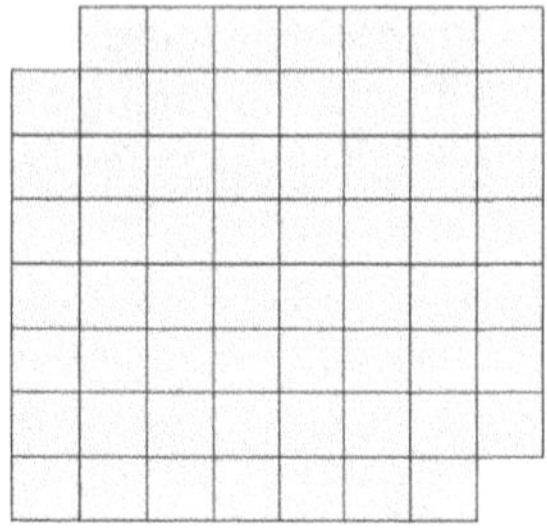

within the given time period, then it will try again with other decisions [14]. Modern solvers learn during such trials for future runs. They also learn from failures, add them as conflicts (no-goods) or as constraints [11, 22]. Thus, they become a bit wiser each time, and the probability that they find a solution faster increases continuously.

## Exercises

**Exercise 7.1** Implement a configurator for the well-known *pigeonhole* problem, in which $p$ pigeons are to be assigned to $h$ holes. Each pigeon must be assigned to exactly one hole, and each hole has place for at most one pigeon.

If $p > h$, the problem is clearly unsatisfiable, but this is not always easy to detect by a solver.

First create a class diagram with cardinalities for the problem, then decide upon variables and values. Implement a declarative encoding (e.g., in MiniZinc), using parameters for the numbers of pigeons and holes. Test for various values, especially with $p = h$ or $p = h + 1$.

How does a solver perform with your encoding for higher numbers? How to improve performance?

**Exercise 7.2** Similarly to Exercise 7.1, implement a configurator for the *tiling* problem and use tuning techniques to improve solving performance (this exercise is more difficult than Exercise 7.1).

The problem consists of filling an $n \times n$ square (without upper-left and lower-right fields) as in Fig. 7.5 with double-square tiles (each tile has either the size $1 \times 2$ or $2 \times 1$). You may produce variants of the problem by reducing or increasing the size of the square, or by changing the position of omitted fields.

**Exercise 7.3** A hardware rack[10] consists of slots, numbered $1 \ldots n$, and modules, which are mounted on slots. Modules have one of two types (sizes): normal (occu-

---

[10] See the beginning of Chap. 2 and the beginning of this chapter for more information on the real-world industrial configuration problem for *hardware racks*.

**Fig. 7.6** A small part of the hardware racks configuration problem (*Source* Own work)

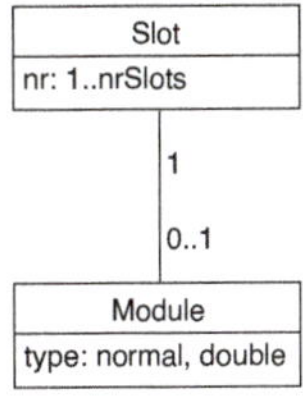


pying one slot) and double (occupying two slots). Modules of the same type can be treated as equivalent (indistinguishable). A UML diagram is depicted in Fig. 7.6.

Input parameters are: number of slots, number of normal modules, and number of double modules. Output is the assignment of modules to slots.

Evaluate the performance of the configurator implementation in the MiniZinc encoding below and improve it by using tuning techniques (or implement a new solution that outperforms it). Provide a table with performance data for the original and your solution on unsatisfiable instance of various sizes (`nrSlots`).

```minizinc
 1  % Input parameters
 2  par int: nrSlots;
 3  par int: nrNormal;
 4  par int: nrDouble;
 5
 6  % Total number of modules
 7  int: nrModules = nrNormal + nrDouble;
 8
 9  % Variables according to UML diagram
10  array [1..nrSlots] of var 0..nrModules:
        slotModule;
11  array [1..nrModules] of var 1..nrSlots:
        moduleSlot;
12  array [1..nrModules] of var bool: moduleDouble;
13
14  % Ensure consistency of bidirectional association
15  constraint forall (m in 1..nrModules) (
16    slotModule[moduleSlot[m]] = m );
17
18  % Double modules occupy two slots
19  constraint forall (m in 1..nrModules) (
20    moduleDouble[m] <->
          slotModule[moduleSlot[m]+1] = m );
21
22  % Ensure required number of double modules
23  constraint nrDouble = sum(m in
          1..nrModules)(moduleDouble[m]);
```

**Exercise 7.4** Calculate and compare complexity metrics (size, constrainedness, etc.) for some of the models in the previous exercises. Do they make sense? You may also extend the model with new functionality and check how the metrics change.

## References


1. Alviano, M., Dodaro, C.: Anytime answer set optimization via unsatisfiable core shrinking. Theory Pract. Log. Program. **16**(5–6), 533–551 (2016). https://doi.org/10.1017/S147106841600020X
2. Beck, K., Beedle, M., van Bennekum, A., Cockburn, A., Cunningham, W., Fowler, M., Grenning, J., Highsmith, J., Hunt, A., Jeffries, R., Kern, J., Marick, B., Martin, R.C., Mellor, S., Schwaber, K., Sutherland, J., Thomas, D.: Manifesto for agile software development (2021). https://agilemanifesto.org
3. Blumöhr, U., Münch, M., Ukalovic, M.: Variant Configuration with SAP, 2nd edn. SAP Press (2011)
4. Carbonnelle, P., Schenner, G., Bruynooghe, M., Bogaerts, B., Denecker, M.: Using symmetries to lift satisfiability checking. In: Wooldridge, M.J., Dy, J.G., Natarajan, S. (eds.) Thirty-Eighth AAAI Conference on Artificial Intelligence, AAAI 2024, Thirty-Sixth Conference on Innovative Applications of Artificial Intelligence, IAAI 2024, Fourteenth Symposium on Educational Advances in Artificial Intelligence, EAAI 2014, February 20–27, 2024, Vancouver, Canada, pp. 7961–7968. AAAI Press (2024). https://doi.org/10.1609/AAAI.V38I8.28633
5. Comploi-Taupe, R., Francescutto, G., Schenner, G.: Applying incremental answer set solving to product configuration. In: Felfernig, A., Fuentes, L., Cleland-Huang, J., Assunção, W.K.G., Quinton, C., Guo, J., Schmid, K., Huchard, M., Ayala, I., Rojas, J.M., Le, V., Horcas, J.M. (eds.) SPLC '22: 26th ACM International Systems and Software Product Line Conference, Graz, Austria, September 12–16, 2022, Vol. B, pp. 150–155. ACM (2022). https://doi.org/10.1145/3503229.3547069
6. Comploi-Taupe, R., Friedrich, G., Schekotihin, K., Weinzierl, A.: Domain-specific heuristics in answer set programming: a declarative non-monotonic approach. J. Artif. Intell. Res. **76**, 59–114 (2023). https://doi.org/10.1613/JAIR.1.14091
7. Falkner, A., Schreiner, H.: SIEMENS: Configuration and reconfiguration in industry. In: Felfernig, A., Hotz, L., Bagley, C., Tiihonen, J. (eds.) Knowledge-based Configuration: From Research to Business Cases, 1st edn. Chap. 16, pp. 199–210. Morgan Kaufmann Publishers Inc., San Francisco, CA, USA (2014)
8. Falkner, A.A., Haselböck, A., Schenner, G., Schreiner, H.: Modeling and solving technical product configuration problems. Artif. Intell. Eng. Des. Anal. Manuf. **25**(2), 115–129 (2011). https://doi.org/10.1017/S0890060410000570
9. Garey, M.R., Johnson, D.S.: Computers and Intractability: A Guide to the Theory of NP-Completeness. W. H, Freeman and Company (1979)
10. Gebser, M., Kaminski, R., Kaufmann, B., Lindauer, M., Ostrowski, M., Romero, J., Schaub, T., Thiele, S., Wanko, P.: Potassco User Guide version 2.2.0 (2019). https://github.com/potassco/guide/releases/tag/v2.2.0
11. Gebser, M., Kaufmann, B., Schaub, T.: Conflict-driven answer set solving: from theory to practice. Artif. Intell. **187**, 52–89 (2012). https://doi.org/10.1016/J.ARTINT.2012.04.001
12. Gomes, C.P., Sellmann, M.: Streamlined constraint reasoning. In: Wallace, M. (ed.) Principles and Practice of Constraint Programming - CP 2004, 10th International Conference, CP 2004, Toronto, Canada, September 27–October 1, 2004, Proceedings, Lecture Notes in Computer Science, vol. 3258, pp. 274–289. Springer, Berlin (2004). https://doi.org/10.1007/978-3-540-30201-8_22
13. Gomes, C.P., Selman, B.: Algorithm portfolios. Artif. Intell. **126**(1), 43–62 (2001). https://doi.org/10.1016/S0004-3702(00)00081-3. Tradeoffs under Bounded Resources
14. Gomes, C.P., Selman, B., Crato, N., Kautz, H.A.: Heavy-tailed phenomena in satisfiability and constraint satisfaction problems. J. Autom. Reason. **24**(1/2), 67–100 (2000). https://doi.org/10.1023/A:1006314320276
15. Haag, A., Haag, L.: Further empowering variant tables for mass customization. Int. J. Ind. Eng. Manag. **10**(2), 155–170 (2019). https://doi.org/10.24867/IJIEM-2019-2-236
16. Karp, R.M.: Reductibility among combinatorial problems. In: Complexity of Computer Computations, pp. 85–103. Plenum Press, New York (1972)

17. Kautz, H.A., Sabharwal, A., Selman, B.: Incomplete algorithms. In: Biere, A., Heule, M., van Maaren, H., Walsh, T. (eds.) Handbook of Satisfiability - Second Edition, Frontiers in Artificial Intelligence and Applications, vol. 336, pp. 213–232. IOS Press (2021). https://doi.org/10.3233/FAIA200989

18. Khalid, I.: Make it work, make it right, make it fast: the evolution of software development (2023). https://medium.com/@ibk9493/make-it-work-make-it-right-make-it-fast-the-evolution-of-software-development-fbbc1eddd33e

19. Korte, B., Vygen, J.: Bin-packing. In: Combinatorial Optimization: Theory and Algorithms, pp. 426–441. Springer, Berlin Heidelberg, Berlin, Heidelberg (2006). https://doi.org/10.1007/3-540-29297-7_18

20. Lawler, E.L., Wood, D.E.: Branch-and-bound methods: a survey. Oper. Res. **14**(4), 699–719 (1966). https://doi.org/10.1287/OPRE.14.4.699

21. Lewis, M., Radbill, D.: Gartner magic quadrant for configure, price and quote applications (2023). https://www.gartner.com/en/documents/5019831

22. Marques-Silva, J., Lynce, I., Malik, S.: Conflict-driven clause learning SAT solvers. In: Biere, A., Heule, M., van Maaren, H., Walsh, T. (eds.) Handbook of Satisfiability, 2nd edn. Frontiers in Artificial Intelligence and Applications, vol. 336, pp. 133–182. IOS Press (2021). https://doi.org/10.3233/FAIA200987

23. Pisinger, D., Ropke, S.: Large neighborhood search. In: Gendreau, M., Potvin, J.Y. (eds.) Handbook of Metaheuristics, pp. 99–127. Springer International Publishing, Cham (2019). https://doi.org/10.1007/978-3-319-91086-4_4

24. Rossi, F., van Beek, P., Walsh, T. (eds.): Handbook of Constraint Programming. Elsevier Science (2006). ISBN 9780080463803. LCCN 2006048518

25. Russell, S., Norvig, P.: Artificial Intelligence: A Modern Approach, 4th edn. Pearson (2020). http://aima.cs.berkeley.edu/

26. Stuckey, P.J., Marriott, K., Tack, G.: The MiniZinc Handbook (2025). https://docs.minizinc.dev/

27. Weinzierl, A., Taupe, R., Friedrich, G.: Advancing lazy-grounding ASP solving techniques–restarts, phase saving, heuristics, and more. Theory Pract. Log. Program. **20**(5), 609–624 (2020). https://doi.org/10.1017/S1471068420000332

28. Wikipedia contributors: Complexity – Wikipedia, the free encyclopedia (2025). https://en.wikipedia.org/w/index.php?title=Complexity&oldid=1304986825

29. Wikipedia contributors: Computational complexity – Wikipedia, the free encyclopedia (2025). https://en.wikipedia.org/w/index.php?title=Computational_complexity&oldid=1312462308

30. Wikipedia contributors: Radar chart – Wikipedia, the free encyclopedia (2025). https://en.wikipedia.org/w/index.php?title=Radar_chart&oldid=1315003120

31. Wolpert, D., Macready, W.: No free lunch theorems for optimization. IEEE Trans. Evol. Comput. **1**(1), 67–82 (1997). https://doi.org/10.1109/4235.585893

32. Zimmerman, B.: Ralph Stacey's agreement & certainty matrix (2001). https://www.nccmt.ca/uploads/media/media/0001/03/219b71c0f7ff72221e90bd4b6b7c537466c18301.pdf

**Open Access** This chapter is licensed under the terms of the Creative Commons Attribution-NonCommercial-NoDerivatives 4.0 International License (http://creativecommons.org/licenses/by-nc-nd/4.0/), which permits any noncommercial use, sharing, distribution and reproduction in any medium or format, as long as you give appropriate credit to the original author(s) and the source, provide a link to the Creative Commons license and indicate if you modified the licensed material. You do not have permission under this license to share adapted material derived from this chapter or parts of it.

The images or other third party material in this chapter are included in the chapter's Creative Commons license, unless indicated otherwise in a credit line to the material. If material is not included in the chapter's Creative Commons license and your intended use is not permitted by statutory regulation or exceeds the permitted use, you will need to obtain permission directly from the copyright holder.

# Chapter 8
# Configuration with Generative AI

Philipp Kogler, Wei Chen, Andreas Falkner, Alois Haselböck, Stefan Wallner, and Richard Comploi-Taupe

**Abstract** The Natural Language Processing (NLP) capabilities of advanced pre-trained Large Language Models (LLMs) have dramatically improved in recent years. This chapter explores the potential of this technology in the context of product configuration through two complementary use cases: In the modeling phase, a copilot can assist users in creating or extending a product model, and in the configuration phase, a copilot can guide users in configuring a product with respect to an existing product model. The technical solution presented in this chapter uses LLMs to formalize constraints from natural language inputs, applies a constraint solver to find a valid configuration with respect to the product model, and communicates the results back to the user in natural language.

A product configurator is a software tool that allows users to configure a product, commonly through a graphical user interface and often in a web-based context. Therefore, interface and interaction design plays a major role in the development of a product configurator but is often overlooked [18]. This observation is especially relevant when complex products are configured by non-expert users. The meaning of configurable components and parameters may not be obvious to those users, which prompts a need for explanation and introduces a learning curve.

A product configurator is almost always an interactive system [4]. A graphical user-interface (GUI) allows users to enter their requirements, which are passed on as input to the constraint solver. The results of the solver are presented on the GUI, and the user can vary or refine their input specification and the solver is called again.

Generative AI enables new possibilities to enhance both the creation of product models and the use of product configurators. As an alternative to GUI-based interactions with product configurators, a configuration copilot [6] offers a text-based chat interface. Using this interface, uninformed users can describe their requirements in natural language without knowledge of the concrete parameters to set and components to select. The copilot then configures the product and responds with a valid

---

This chapter is based on the paper *Configuration Copilot: Towards Integrating Large Language Models and Constraints* from the Configuration Workshop 2024 [6], which has been shortened in some parts, extended in others, and has generally been revised for the purpose of serving as a chapter of this book. The original paper is licensed under CC BY 4.0.

---

© Siemens Aktiengesellschaft Österreich 2026

R. Comploi-Taupe and A. Falkner, *Product Configuration*,
SpringerBriefs in Computer Science,
https://doi.org/10.1007/978-3-032-17163-4_8

configuration complying with the initial requirements. The user can interactively refine the product configuration.

In addition to assisting end users in the configuration process, generative AI can also support the creation of product models themselves. A modeling copilot can assist product modelers, engineers, and domain experts in developing or formalizing product models, extracting constraints from specifications, and maintaining configuration knowledge bases.

To realize these AI-assisted configuration and modeling copilots, pre-trained Large Language Models (LLMs) are commonly used for the processing of natural language. Recent advances in this field have enabled use cases that require the understanding and generation of not only natural language but also code. Well-known limitations include a lack of reliability, guaranteed correctness, domain-specific knowledge in general-purpose LLMs, and limited reasoning abilities [13]. These limitations are highly relevant for product configuration as the correctness of resulting configurations is especially important. Therefore, LLMs alone are typically not sufficient, and are not a replacement for traditional configuration engines.

The following sections discuss how LLMs can still be used reliably for product configuration and how the shortcomings of LLMs can be addressed with neuro-symbolic approaches that combine LLMs with logical reasoning. While the strengths of LLMs lie in natural language understanding and generation, the reasoning over product models and constraints is handled by logic-based reasoners such as constraint solvers.

## 8.1 Large Language Models and Their Application in Product Configuration

Pre-training task-agnostic aspects of natural language processing (NLP) tasks is a central concept of LLMs. The *Transformer* architecture enables this approach on a large scale through parallelization. Transformer models are able to capture complex patterns and long-range dependencies in texts through the multi-head self-attention mechanism. Compared to previous state-of-the-art models such as recurrent neural networks (RNNs) or long short-term memory networks (LSTMs) a performance improvement in various NLP tasks is observed [11, 17].

*Decoder-only* models are a subclass of transformer-based architectures and are primarily used for sequence-to-sequence tasks such as translation. Auto-regressive models predict the next single token (sub-word) by maximizing the log-likelihood given all previous words and the model parameters [17].

The size and quality of the pre-training corpus have a strong impact on performance [11]. LLMs are trained on publicly available data and excel in general language tasks. Highly specialized tasks require expert knowledge that is often not included in the training data, and therefore LLMs may not be able to generate accurate output.

## Challenges of Using LLMs for Product Configuration

Three main challenges to consider when using LLMs for product configuration are [8, 9]:

- Domain-specific knowledge: Pre-trained LLMs are a general-purpose solution. They lack specific knowledge about the domain, the product, and the language of the configurator.
- Probabilistic system: A specific output format, compliance with a given product model, and satisfaction of given constraints are generally not guaranteed.
- Reasoning: While LLMs, especially so-called reasoning models, show traits of human-like reasoning, they do not perform true and reliable logical reasoning but rather rely on pattern matching and statistical inference.

Domain-specific knowledge can be introduced to a general-purpose LLM through domain customization by employing techniques like *prompting* or *in-context learning* and *fine-tuning* [9]. *Prompts* are task-specific input texts, and *prompt engineering* is the technique of carefully designing prompts to guide the LLM towards a desired output. Prompts are limited in length, and therefore often do not fit the whole product model, especially in more complex enterprise environments. To mitigate this issue, retrieval-augmented generation (RAG) can be employed. In general, a RAG system queries an external knowledge base to enrich a prompt with relevant contextual information, for example with relevant parts of a product model. *Fine-tuning* is the technique of applying additional training on a smaller, more specialized dataset to a pre-trained model to enhance its performance in a specific domain. For an LLM to learn a product model through fine-tuning, much more data (e.g., hundreds or thousands of examples of natural-language inputs and expected outputs) is needed compared to in-context learning [8, 9]. Due to a lack of high-quality training data, and the necessity to fine-tune a separate model for each product, fine-tuning is often not feasible.

While the probabilistic nature and limited reasoning abilities are fundamental limitations of LLMs that cannot be easily lifted, they can be mitigated. The core idea is to use the LLM for natural language processing, and to use a logic-based configuration engine for reasoning over the product model. To make the communication between the LLM and the reasoner more reliable, natural language can be formalized to a structured intermediate representation that later serves as the input for the configuration engine. The following two paragraphs describe techniques that enable reliable cooperation between the two components.

## Domain-Specific Intermediate Language

The use of intermediate representations in code generation has been explored across various domains to improve the correctness of the translation from high-level specifications in natural language to a target programming language, e.g., a formal representation of requirements or constraints [7].

Rather than generating constraints directly in a specific constraint language, an intermediate JSON-based representation for product configuration can be used. This approach addresses several limitations of directly generating the target constraint language using an LLM. First, JSON is widely represented in LLM training corpora compared to specialized constraint languages that appear infrequently in training data, which would negatively impact the correctness of the output [2]. Second, this approach decouples the LLM from the specific constraint language, making the system agnostic of the underlying configuration engine. And third, the use of an intermediate JSON allows the creation of product-specific JSON schemas. By encoding product-specific property names, parameter types, and valid value ranges as enumerations, a standard JSON validator can check whether the LLM-generated JSON representation is correct and complies with the product model. The JSON schema thus formalizes the product family and corresponds to the configuration model (L1) in the representation layers in Chap. 4.

## *Grammar-Constrained Decoding*

As an extension to the validation of a product-specific JSON-based representation, grammar-constrained decoding is a technique that further improves reliability. While a standard JSON validator checks the compliance of a JSON instance against a schema after it has been generated, and thus introduces validation-retry-loops to the generation process, grammar-constrained decoding ensures on-the-fly that the LLM is restricted to only generate valid instances complying with the given schema.

We now describe the technical implementation of a post-processor, as depicted in Fig. 8.1, that realizes grammar-constrained-decoding for JSON-based representations using a JSON schema for a specific product family:

As an auto-regressive Transformer model generates its output step-by-step as tokens, the post-processor engages into every generation step: For each step, the

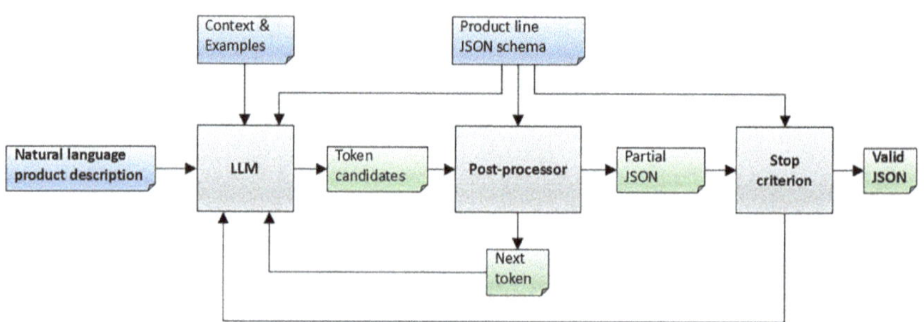


**Fig. 8.1** Detail view of the post-processing technique (*Source* [6])

LLM generates a list of candidates for the next token based on the prompt and the generated output so far. Sorted by priority as evaluated by the LLM, the post-processor determines whether the token candidate represents a valid continuation of the partial output sequence (partial intermediate JSON). The valid token candidate with the highest priority is then selected, handed back to the LLM, and added to the partial JSON, extending it one step further. A completeness checker determines after every step if the JSON is complete [8].

The JSON-based intermediate language is formally defined by a JSON schema specification and the post-processor is therefore a specialized JSON validator that can strictly validate any partial JSON against the schema. This implementation is based on deterministic finite automata (DFA). Each generic JSON language element (object, list, string, number, etc.) is represented by a DFA, keeping track of the current state. The token generated by the LLM is broken down to single-character inputs for the JSON validator. Depending on the schema and the current state, only a set of characters is accepted. If a character is rejected, the current token is considered invalid, and the validator state is rolled back to the last valid token. State changes are triggered by characters until the final state is reached. When the DFA reaches its final state, the generated valid JSON is complete [8].

## 8.2  Modeling Copilot

While the main focus of this chapter is the configuration copilot discussed in Sect. 8.3, we briefly mention another application of generative AI to product configuration: a modeling copilot. By this we mean LLM-assisted generation of product models, i.e., configuration knowledge bases including constraints.

Let us consider our running example: The vendor of folding bikes might decide to offer frames in more than one size in the future. A modeling copilot could be used to extend both the data structures (the Frame class in the PLM/Engineering view in Fig. 3.5 in Chap. 3 needs to be extended by an additional attribute along with an appropriate domain) and the constraints (the CRM/Sales constraints in the same example would need to restrict the choice of frame size depending on the customer's height), all of which could be automatically translated to MiniZinc data structures and constraints.

To the best of our knowledge, a modeling copilot for configurable product models does not yet exist. However, there has been some research in the direction of LLM-assisted knowledge base construction [5, 10, 14–16].

## 8.3  Configuration Copilot

This section describes the specific technical approach used for the configuration copilot that enables product configuration through natural language.

**Fig. 8.2** Architecture of the configuration copilot (*Source* [6])

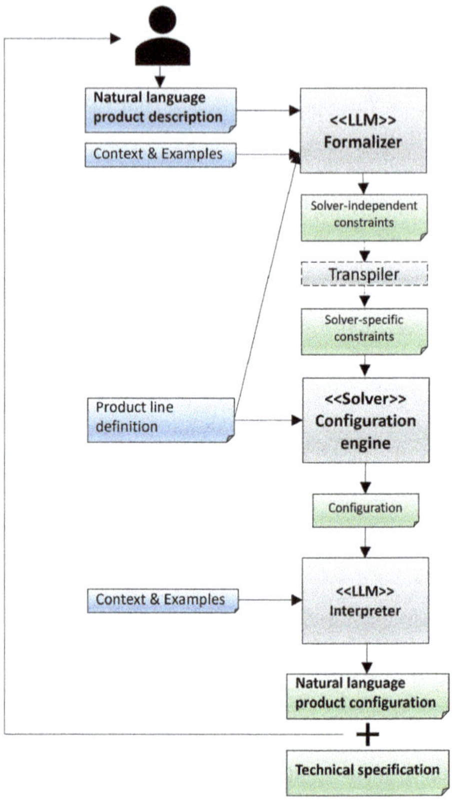


Figure 8.2 shows an overview of the architecture. A user configures a product by providing a natural-language description of their requirements. The Formalizer (see below and detailed in Fig. 8.1) is a specialized LLM-based component that translates the requirements to constraints. The Configuration Engine is a constraint solver that attempts to find a configuration that satisfies the general constraints of the product line combined with the user constraints provided by the Formalizer. An Interpreter (see below) translates the configuration back to natural language. The configuration copilot then responds with a natural-language description of the configured product accompanied by the full technical specification (product configuration as determined by the Configuration Engine). The user can then further refine the product configuration interactively.

Note the similarity of this architecture and our general configuration process (cf. Fig. 1.4 in Chap. 1) as well as to the solving process in declarative programming (e.g., Fig. 5.4 in Chap. 5).

## *Formalizer*

The input to the Formalizer is a natural-language description of arbitrary product requirements provided by a non-expert. Utilizing the NLP capabilities of LLMs, the formalization can be viewed as a sequence-to-sequence translation task from natural language to a formal specification. The LLM is tasked with natural language understanding and the identification of corresponding parameters or components of the product (line), but is specifically not tasked with reasoning (e.g., constraint satisfaction).

The Formalizer addresses domain customization and reliable output generation through few-shot prompting and algorithmic post-processing [8]. Few-shot prompting has been shown to effectively extend the capabilities of LLMs with domain knowledge while requiring significantly less training data than fine-tuning [1]. Knowledge of the product line is incorporated through a system prompt describing the product line with its parameters and components. A small set of examples is appended as pairs of natural-language inputs and expected outputs to provide the LLM with more context and guide it towards the expected behavior.

Rather than generating output directly in a specific constraint language, an intermediate JSON-based language is used, which can then be easily transpiled.[1] The Transpiler parses the JSON constraint representation and maps its elements to corresponding constructs of the specific constraint language (e.g., MiniZinc) following predefined rules.

## *Configuration Engine*

Given the user constraints combined with the complete product line definition, the Configuration Engine evaluates whether the constraints are satisfiable and returns a configuration. The product line as well as the user constraints are modeled in MiniZinc [12]. The solver returns the full product configuration as a list of variable assignments which serves as an input to the Interpreter. For details on using MiniZinc and other Constraint Programming (CP) languages for product configuration, we refer to Chap. 5.

## *Interpreter*

The Interpreter is an LLM module that explains the product configuration found by the Configuration Engine. The goal is to provide the user with a less technical summary that is understandable for non-experts.

---

[1] This corresponds to using JSON as the standard language for an Exporter in our reference architecture (Sect. 3.4) to avoid vendor lock-in (cf. Sect. 3.3).

Prompting is sufficient for this use case as LLMs generally perform well in the translation from a formal specification to a natural-language summary as all facts are directly present in the prompt. The context given to the LLM consists of three aspects: General instructions for the LLM what to do,[2] the product line definition, and examples. The LLM is prompted to evaluate which properties and components are most important to be included in the summary. This is achieved by adding importance hints to the product line definition, and by appending the original user input. Properties and components mentioned directly in the user input are given more importance and are more likely to be included in the summary. The result is a more natural context-aware explanation of the most relevant aspects in the product configuration.

## 8.4  Practical Aspects and Evaluation

The application of Large Language Models (LLMs) as copilots for product modeling and configuration requires considerations of multiple practical aspects beyond the conceptual architecture. This includes the selection of a pre-trained base model, the domain customization of the model, and the deployment.

The capabilities of LLMs depend strongly on the pre-training corpus and model size [8]. Larger models typically achieve stronger performance [8] but impose significant hardware requirements or API costs for model inference or fine-tuning.

Even though LLMs are trained on a large variety of tasks, their performance for one specific task, e.g. product modeling or configuration, cannot be guaranteed without a formal evaluation. Therefore, an important aspect of employing LLMs for product modeling or configuration is the evaluation of multiple LLMs for this specific use case. The most essential step to be evaluated is the understanding of user intent (natural language) and its correct formalization to the intermediate domain-specific language (DSL) for product configuration (Formalizer). The transpilation of the intermediate DSL to the target language (e.g., MiniZinc) is done by a deterministic transpiler, and the reasoning is done by the configuration engine (constraint solver), and are therefore out of scope for the evaluation of the LLM (see Chap. 6 for quality aspects in this area). The Interpreter is merely a less critical summarization of provided data, a task that LLMs typically excel at, and is therefore also omitted from this evaluation.

In the evaluation of LLMs, commonly used metrics typically compare the generated output with pre-defined expected output for a specific input based on text similarity, for instance using the well-known *BLEU* score. However, the Formalizer does not generate natural language, but a structured intermediate DSL that closely resembles code. Text-based similarity metrics are therefore unsuitable, as they simply compute similarity between two texts, but not functional equivalence. Two code snippets can be different in pure text, but be functionally equivalent. On the other

---

[2] E.g., the instructions comprise an introduction to product configuration and a description of the task to translate natural-language input of a user to formal requirements in a configuration DSL.

hand, two code snippets can only have a minor textual difference but differ drastically in functionality [3].

Thus, a specific metric is needed that adequately captures functional equivalency. See the paper by Kogler et al. [6] for details on how to compute a similarity metric from matching configuration parameters and their values. This paper also includes an evaluation based on this metric that compares the similarity scores among several LLMs.

For deployment, open-source LLMs can be self-hosted, or cloud offerings can be used via APIs. Self-hosted LLMs typically allow for more fine-grained control over the inference or fine-tuning process. The described technique of grammar-constrained decoding is therefore easily possible either through standard libraries or custom implementations for specific use cases. Cloud offerings via APIs are typically significantly less flexible, but easier to start with as no self-managed hardware for model inference or fine-tuning is needed. Data privacy and security are further concerns to be considered when using cloud offerings.

## Example

Returning to the folding bike example, a user of the configuration copilot (Sect. 8.3) would start by describing their requirements for a folding bike in natural language.

```
1  I am 1.85 meters tall, and I want my folding bike to be offroad-capable, but I
       don't need any reflectors.
2  I also don't want a leather saddle.
```

This natural-language description is then formalized to the intermediate JSON language. The Formalizer knows the configurable properties and their format, but does not know the constraints of the product model. Therefore, it cannot reason over the product model and only formalizes the user requirements.[3]

```
1  {
2      "customer_height": {
3          "operator": "equals",
4          "value": 185
5      },
6      "offroad": {
7          "operator": "equals",
8          "value": true
9      },
10      "reflectors": [
11      {
12          "operator": "equals",
13          "value": false
```

---

[3] For example, the input "I am 1.85 m tall" is translated to a JSON structure expressing that the customer height attribute is equal to 185, and the input "I don't need any reflectors" is translated to two structures each individually setting the reflectors of one wheel to false.

```
14        },
15        {
16            "operator": "equals",
17            "value": false
18        }
19        ],
20        "saddle_material": {
21            "operator": "not_equals",
22            "value": "leather"
23        }
24  }
```

This list of solver-independent constraints is then directly transpiled to solver-specific constraints. These are not product constraints, but constraints representing customer requirements (cf. Sect. 5.5).

```
1  constraint customer_height = 185;
2  constraint offroad = True;
3  constraint forall (i in 1..2) (reflectors[i] =
       False);
4  constraint saddle_material != leather;
```

Together with the full constraint model (product line definition), the Configuration Engine evaluates the constraints and returns a full product configuration of the folding bike for the specific user requirements as a list of value assignments to the configurable parameters. The Configuration Engine considers user requirements (e.g., *the saddle material must not be leather*), as well as constraints defined in the product model (e.g., *the customer height is 185cm, therefore the seat post must be 'extended'*, or *the offroad option is selected, therefore the mudguards must be selected*—see the Example in Chap. 3), and picks reasonable values for unspecified properties (e.g., frame material). The Interpreter converts this configuration back to natural language and returns it to the user.

```
1  Your folding bike has a steel frame with mudguards, an extended seat post with a
       synthetic seat material, and marathon wheels without reflectors.
2
3  Here is the full technical configuration:
4
5  frame.material = steel
6  frame.mudguard = True
7  seat.saddle_material = synthetic
8  seat.seatpost = extended
9  wheel[1].type = marathon
10 wheel[2].reflectors = False
11 wheel[1].type = marathon
12 wheel[1].reflectors = False
13 (...)
```

## Exercises

**Exercise 8.1** Let us assume that a bike shop owner does not have a configurator for their offering (which can be described by the text in Exercise 4.6) but only the following list of sold configurations:

- city bike, light (40 times)
- city bike, e-motor, light (20 times)
- mountain bike (25 times)
- mountain bike, e-motor, light (5 times)
- racing bike (30 times)
- sport use, mountain bike (25 times)
- sport use, off-road, mountain bike (5 times)
- sport use, racing bike (10 times)

They ponder using an LLM (e.g., ChatGPT) to assist customers to select a bicycle, just based on this list:

- Can an LLM warn about wrong configurations, such as racing bike with e-motor, or city bike without light, or night use without light?
- Can an LLM recommend a valid configuration based on user requirements, such as city bike with e-motor, or sport use at night, or sport use on road?
- How can the quality of this approach be improved?

**Exercise 8.2** Given the same setting as in Exercise 8.1: How will a hybrid approach as presented in Sect. 8.3 perform? Sketch some sample user sessions.

## References

1. Brown, T., Mann, B., Ryder, N., Subbiah, M., Kaplan, J.D., Dhariwal, P., Neelakantan, A., Shyam, P., Sastry, G., Askell, A., Agarwal, S., Herbert-Voss, A., Krueger, G., Henighan, T., Child, R., Ramesh, A., Ziegler, D., Wu, J., Winter, C., Hesse, C., Chen, M., Sigler, E., Litwin, M., Gray, S., Chess, B., Clark, J., Berner, C., McCandlish, S., Radford, A., Sutskever, I., Amodei, D.: Language models are few-shot learners. In: Larochelle, H., Ranzato, M., Hadsell, R., Balcan, M., Lin, H. (eds.) Advances in Neural Information Processing Systems, vol. 33, pp. 1877–1901. Curran Associates, Inc. (2020). https://proceedings.neurips.cc/paper_files/paper/2020/file/1457c0d6bfcb4967418bfb8ac142f64a-Paper.pdf
2. Cassano, F., Gouwar, J., Lucchetti, F., Schlesinger, C., Freeman, A., Anderson, C.J., Feldman, M.Q., Greenberg, M., Jangda, A., Guha, A.: Knowledge transfer from high-resource to low-resource programming languages for code LLMS. Proc. ACM Program. Lang. **8**(OOPSLA2) (2024). https://doi.org/10.1145/3689735
3. Chen, M., Tworek, J., Jun, H., Yuan, Q., Ponde, H., Kaplan, J., Edwards, H., Burda, Y., Joseph, N., Brockman, G., Ray, A., Puri, R., Krueger, G., Petrov, M., Khlaaf, H., Sastry, G., Mishkin, P., Chan, B., Gray, S., Ryder, N., Pavlov, M., Power, A., Kaiser, L., Bavarian, M., Winter, C., Tillet, P., Such, F.P., Cummings, D.W., Plappert, M., Chantzis, F., Barnes, E., Herbert-Voss, A., Guss, W.H., Nichol, A., Babuschkin, I., Balaji, S.A., Jain, S., Carr, A., Leike, J., Achiam, J., Misra, V., Morikawa, E., Radford, A., Knight, M.M., Brundage, M., Murati, M., Mayer, K., Welinder, P., McGrew, B., Amodei, D., McCandlish, S., Sutskever, I., Zaremba, W.: Evaluating large language models trained on code (2021). arXiv:2107.03374

4. Falkner, A.A., Haselböck, A., Krames, G., Schenner, G., Schreiner, H., Taupe, R.: Solver requirements for interactive configuration. J. Univers. Comput. Sci. **26**(3), 343–373 (2020). http://www.jucs.org/jucs_26_3/solver_requirements_for_interactive
5. Hotz, L., Bähnisch, C., Lubos, S., Felfernig, A., Haag, A., Twiefel, J.: Exploiting large language models for the automated generation of constraint satisfaction problems. In: Vareilles, É., Grosso, C., Horcas, J.M., Felfernig, A. (eds.) Proceedings of the 26th International Workshop on Configuration (ConfWS 2024) co-located with the 30th International Conference on Principles and Practice of Constraint Programming (CP 2024), Girona, Spain, September 2–3, 2024, CEUR Workshop Proceedings, vol. 3812, pp. 91–100. CEUR-WS.org (2024). https://ceur-ws.org/Vol-3812/paper13.pdf
6. Kogler, P., Chen, W., Falkner, A.A., Haselböck, A., Wallner, S.: Configuration copilot: towards integrating large language models and constraints. In: Vareilles, É., Grosso, C., Horcas, J.M., Felfernig, A. (eds.) Proceedings of the 26th International Workshop on Configuration (ConfWS 2024) co-located with the 30th International Conference on Principles and Practice of Constraint Programming (CP 2024), Girona, Spain, September 2–3, 2024, CEUR Workshop Proceedings, vol. 3812, pp. 101–110. CEUR-WS.org (2024). https://ceur-ws.org/Vol-3812/paper14.pdf
7. Kogler, P., Chen, W., Wallner, S.: Code generation for niche programming languages with large language models. In: SE 2024 - Companion. Gesellschaft für Informatik, Bonn (2025). https://doi.org/10.18420/se2025-ws-13
8. Kogler, P., Falkner, A., Sperl, S.: Reliable generation of formal specifications using large language models. In: SE 2024 - Companion, pp. 141–153. Gesellschaft für Informatik e.V. (2024). https://doi.org/10.18420/sw2024-ws_10
9. Ling, C., Zhao, X., Lu, J., Deng, C., Zheng, C., Wang, J., Chowdhury, T., Li, Y., Cui, H., Zhang, X., Zhao, T., Panalkar, A., Cheng, W., Wang, H., Liu, Y., Chen, Z., Chen, H., White, C., Gu, Q., Yang, C., Zhao, L.: Beyond one-model-fits-all: a survey of domain specialization for large language models. CoRR (2023). https://doi.org/10.48550/ARXIV.2305.18703, arXiv:2305.18703
10. Michailidis, K., Tsouros, D., Guns, T.: Constraint modelling with llms using in-context learning. In: Shaw, P. (ed.) 30th International Conference on Principles and Practice of Constraint Programming, CP 2024, September 2–6, 2024, Girona, Spain, LIPIcs, vol. 307, pp. 20:1–20:27. Schloss Dagstuhl - Leibniz-Zentrum für Informatik (2024). https://doi.org/10.4230/LIPICS.CP.2024.20
11. Min, B., Ross, H., Sulem, E., Veyseh, A.P.B., Nguyen, T.H., Sainz, O., Agirre, E., Heintz, I., Roth, D.: Recent advances in natural language processing via large pre-trained language models: a survey. ACM Comput. Surv. **56**(2), 30:1–30:40 (2024). https://doi.org/10.1145/3605943
12. Nethercote, N., Stuckey, P.J., Becket, R., Brand, S., Duck, G.J., Tack, G.: MiniZinc: Towards a standard CP modelling language. In: Bessiere, C. (ed.) Principles and Practice of Constraint Programming - CP 2007, 13th International Conference, CP 2007, Providence, RI, USA, September 23–27, 2007, Proceedings, Lecture Notes in Computer Science, vol. 4741, pp. 529–543. Springer, Berlin (2007). https://doi.org/10.1007/978-3-540-74970-7_38
13. Nijkamp, E., Pang, B., Hayashi, H., Tu, L., Wang, H., Zhou, Y., Savarese, S., Xiong, C.: CodeGen: an open large language model for code with multi-turn program synthesis. In: The Eleventh International Conference on Learning Representations, ICLR 2023, Kigali, Rwanda, May 1–5, 2023. OpenReview.net (2023). https://openreview.net/forum?id=iaYcJKpY2B_
14. Penco, R., Pintar, D., Vranić, M., Šoštarić, M.: Large language model-driven framework for automated constraint model generation in configuration problems. Appl. Sci. **15**(12) (2025). https://doi.org/10.3390/app15126518

15. Szeider, S.: Bridging language models and symbolic solvers via the model context protocol. In: Berg, J., Nordström, J. (eds.) 28th International Conference on Theory and Applications of Satisfiability Testing (SAT 2025), Leibniz International Proceedings in Informatics (LIPIcs), vol. 341, pp. 30:1–30:12. Schloss Dagstuhl - Leibniz-Zentrum für Informatik, Dagstuhl, Germany (2025). https://drops.dagstuhl.de/entities/document/10.4230/LIPIcs.SAT.2025.30

16. Tsouros, D.C., Verhaeghe, H., Kadioglu, S., Guns, T.: Holy grail 2.0: from natural language to constraint models. CoRR (2023). arXiv:abs/2308.01589. https://doi.org/10.48550/ARXIV.2308.01589

17. Vaswani, A., Shazeer, N., Parmar, N., Uszkoreit, J., Jones, L., Gomez, A.N., Kaiser, L.u., Polosukhin, I.: Attention is all you need. In: Guyon, I., Luxburg, U.V., Bengio, S., Wallach, H., Fergus, R., Vishwanathan, S., Garnett, R. (eds.) Advances in Neural Information Processing Systems, vol. 30. Curran Associates, Inc. (2017). https://proceedings.neurips.cc/paper_files/paper/2017/file/3f5ee243547dee91fbd053c1c4a845aa-Paper.pdf

18. Yi, M., Huang, Z., Yu, Y.: Creating a sustainable e-commerce environment: the impact of product configurator interaction design on consumer personalized customization experience. Sustainability **14**(23) (2022). https://www.mdpi.com/2071-1050/14/23/15903

**Open Access** This chapter is licensed under the terms of the Creative Commons Attribution-NonCommercial-NoDerivatives 4.0 International License (http://creativecommons.org/licenses/by-nc-nd/4.0/), which permits any noncommercial use, sharing, distribution and reproduction in any medium or format, as long as you give appropriate credit to the original author(s) and the source, provide a link to the Creative Commons license and indicate if you modified the licensed material. You do not have permission under this license to share adapted material derived from this chapter or parts of it.

The images or other third party material in this chapter are included in the chapter's Creative Commons license, unless indicated otherwise in a credit line to the material. If material is not included in the chapter's Creative Commons license and your intended use is not permitted by statutory regulation or exceeds the permitted use, you will need to obtain permission directly from the copyright holder.

# Chapter 9
# Sustainability-Aware Product Configuration

Gottfried Schenner, Giray Havur, Sophie Rogenhofer, Stefan Wallner, Erwin Filtz, Tassilo Pellegrini, Andreas Falkner, and Richard Comploi-Taupe

**Abstract** The incorporation of sustainability and lifecycle information is an important aspect of modern product configurators. In this chapter, we describe how to enhance a classic component-based product configuration model by integrating sustainability and lifecycle data. We also identify the relevant external data sources—such as lifecycle assessment databases, product lifecycle management systems, and environmental product declarations—that provide the necessary input. Using a prototypical MiniZinc implementation, we demonstrate how to estimate lifecycle indicators when precise values are unavailable.

What is sustainability, and why is it relevant for product configuration?

A single specific definition of sustainability may never be possible. But the concept is still useful. Let's say that sustainability means meeting our own needs without compromising the ability of future generations to meet their own needs [27]. Usually, three dimensions of sustainability are considered: environmental, social, and economic.

We focus here on the environmental dimension. The environment is currently facing major issues: global warming, pollution, and biodiversity collapse. Burning fossil fuels warms the planet. Pollution includes air pollution, (micro)plastic in the ocean and everywhere else, chemicals, and pesticides. Biodiversity collapse means the extinction of many species and the destruction of rainforests.

In 2015, it was agreed to limit the rise in mean global temperature with respect to pre-industrial levels to well below $2\,°C$, preferably to $1.5\,°C$ [7]. Global warming is caused by emitting greenhouse gases such as $CO_2$. Energy use in the manufacturing industry accounts for approximately 24% of global greenhouse gas emissions (even excluding transport and usage phase) [19]. Companies need to address the environmental impact of their products due to societal responsibility, public pressure, regulations (such as $CO_2$ taxes), and also to achieve a competitive advantage, since "eco-friendly" products are in high demand.

---

This chapter is based on the paper *A lifecycle- and sustainability-aware product configuration model for modular industrial systems* from the Configuration Workshop 2025 [20], which has been shortened in some parts, extended in others, and has generally been revised for the purpose of serving as a chapter of this book. The original paper is licensed under CC BY 4.0.

---

© Siemens Aktiengesellschaft Österreich 2026

R. Comploi-Taupe and A. Falkner, *Product Configuration*,
SpringerBriefs in Computer Science,
https://doi.org/10.1007/978-3-032-17163-4_9

Building on the Green Deal [3] and its sub-policy, the Circular Economy Action Plan (CEAP) [4], the Clean Industrial Deal of the European Union (EU) aims to address climate and environmental challenges while enhancing Europe's competitiveness and promoting a cleaner, more sustainable future. This also affects industry and industrial production, and from a product configuration point-of-view, the Ecodesign for Sustainable Products Regulation (ESPR) [18] needs to be considered in the product configuration phase. To comply with upcoming legal requirements established through delegated domain- and sector-specific acts complementing the ESPR, methods for measuring and documenting product sustainability indicators, such as ISO-certified, LCA-based Product Environmental Footprints (PEFs) or corresponding Environmental Product Declarations (EPDs), will eventually become mandatory in the EU. According to the ESPR, sustainability-related product information must be provided through a Digital Product Passport (DPP), which aims to facilitate more circular product and material flows by promoting transparency, accountability, and environmental governance throughout a product's lifecycle.

Following this trend in the product configuration community, the term "green configuration" [9] has been established, referring to a product customization service which also considers sustainability aspects, e.g., in the form of carbon footprinting. Several vendors of CPQ solutions (cf. Sect. 5.6), such as CAS Merlin,[1] encoway,[2] or Tacton[3] are already integrating green configuration capabilities into their offerings.

We argue that lifecycle-related product characteristics—such as total cost of ownership, environmental impact, repairability, reusability, and recyclability—should be considered during the configuration phase. So far, the problem has been acknowledged and theoretically analyzed from various angles (e.g., [1, 9, 15, 26]). In this chapter, we discuss how a green configuration model differs from a traditional configuration model based on an example from the industry sector. We develop a conceptual product configuration model enriched with sustainability and circularity information, which helps us to identify the challenges for getting the information from external sources like sustainability databases or product lifecycle management (PLM) systems. Additionally, we show how to encode the conceptual model in MiniZinc [17] (cf. Sect. 5.5).

## 9.1 State of the Art

In the following section, we summarize the state-of-the-art and introduce the most important concepts.

---

[1] https://www.green-configuration.de/.

[2] https://www.encoway.de/blog/green-configuration/.

[3] https://global.tacton.com/products/tacton-cpq/environmental-footprint-configuration/.

## *Green Configuration*

Green Configuration represents an innovative approach that combines conventional product configuration systems with environmental impact assessments while incorporating circular economy principles such as recyclability, repairability, and reusability. By providing immediate feedback on environmental consequences of configuration choices, stakeholders are enabled to make informed decisions. This approach supports the transition toward more environmentally conscious product designs and circular business models, optimizing resource efficiency and minimizing waste throughout the product lifecycle.

One prominent example of environmental impact assessment used in Green Configuration is Life Cycle Assessment (LCA) [2]. LCA is an ISO-certified methodology [13, 14] that evaluates environmental impacts throughout a product's complete lifecycle—from raw material extraction through manufacturing, distribution, and use, to final disposal or recycling. The process encompasses detailed analysis of energy and material flows across supply and value chains, calculating associated environmental impacts and emissions. LCAs are fundamentally based on Bill of Materials (BOM) and Bill of Processes (BOP) throughout a product's lifecycle. For decades, LCA has served as the standard for environmental impact assessment according to ISO 14040, with results typically documented in Environmental Product Declarations (EPDs) following ISO 14025. Traditionally, LCA methodologies have operated independently from product configuration processes.

Recent research in green configuration has focused on describing requirements and architectures for integrating LCA into product configurators. Comploi-Taupe et al. [9] have identified four key architectural approaches for combining configurators, knowledge bases, and LCA tools:

1. Sequential Approach: LCA is performed manually after configuration.
2. Loosely Coupled Architecture: Automated but separate LCA calculations requiring synchronization between configurator and LCA tool.
3. Tightly Coupled Architecture: Configurator manages LCA data and directly interfaces with the LCA tool, providing a unified interface.
4. Integrated Architecture: LCA calculation is fully embedded within the configurator, enabling direct environmental data usage during reasoning and optimization.

While the integrated approach offers the most seamless user experience, it demands significant development resources and continuous maintenance to ensure compliance with standards.

Wiezorek and Christensen [26] follow a similar argumentation line that configurators and LCA tools must be integrated and propose extensions to existing product configurators to support green configuration. Jakobsen et al. [15] go one step further and argue that the sustainability aspect already needs to be considered in the product configurator design phase and provide a comprehensive overview of product configurator architectures and sustainable product configuration systems.

## *Legal*

Although product configuration can be seen as a purely technical task of combining different components to fulfill technical and user requirements (constraints), it is also necessary to consider legal requirements in the configuration process, if they were not already addressed in the product design phase. Such legal requirements are not limited to isolated aspects of product configuration but cover different topics, such as information and documentation requirements, restrictions on the usage of hazardous materials, or the disassembling and disposal of products. Additionally, there might be no single legal framework to be considered in a particular product configuration project but multiple national and international legal frameworks.

The rising importance of sustainability and related topics has also triggered regulatory activities from the European Union. All of the regulatory acts are supporting overarching goals as laid out in the Clean Industrial Deal [6] and its sub-policies fostering climate-neutrality and the reduction of greenhouse gas emissions. Of special interest for industry is the Green Deal Industrial Plan [5], which aims to simplify the regulatory environment, get easier and faster access to funding, enable the improvement of skills, and foster fair and open trade. Another regulatory framework is the Ecodesign for Sustainable Products Regulation (ESPR) [18] focusing on improving circularity, durability, and energy performance by defining ecodesign requirements to better meet the material and procedural demands of circular product design and end-of-life handling. Measures are laid out in the ESPR to achieve these requirements, such as the Digital Product Passport (DPP), which serves as a digital identity for products (including components).

In addition to regulatory acts from different legislative bodies, there are also activities from standardization organizations, for instance the International Standardization Organization (ISO) to be considered. The standards ISO 14020 and 14025 are relevant for the generation of Environmental Product Declarations, ISO 59040 is dealing with circular economy, and ISO 59014 with material sustainability.

We refer to the paper on which this chapter is based [20] for more details on legal aspects.

## *Data Sources for Green Configuration*

Product configuration typically relies on multiple interconnected data sources that provide the structural, commercial, and logical foundation required to define and validate a specific product variant. In configuration environments, especially those aligned with sustainability goals, these core data categories are increasingly complemented by sustainability and lifecycle data. We focus here on sustainability and lifecycle data, while other data categories are covered by other chapters and are also detailed in the paper this chapter is based upon [20].

In addition to data for traditional product configuration, Green Configuration requires sustainability and lifecycle data as a crucial data category that captures key environmental and circular economy-related information. This data category can include various environmental impact metrics such as carbon footprint, energy and water consumption, and material toxicity. It also might cover circular economy aspects like recyclability rates, material recovery potential, and product durability. Additionally, it encompasses regulatory compliance information, including supplier declarations and certifications. Such data can be sourced from various providers and is increasingly critical for aligning product configurations with sustainability goals and legal requirements. However, significant challenges remain in the practical implementation of these data sources. Many companies do not yet disclose environmental data for their products, partly because they do not know them themselves. This results in missing environmental data concerning the supply chain, usage, and end-of-life processing. Furthermore, the required data is often incomplete, with some components needing to be manually disassembled and weighed because suppliers do not provide corresponding data. The calculation of lifecycle assessments relies on comprehensive databases that contain environmental impact data for materials, processes, and energy flows. Key databases include Sphera (GaBi),[4] which provides detailed lifecycle inventory data for thousands of materials and processes across industries. The ecoinvent database[5] is another widely used source. These databases include information on greenhouse gas emissions, resource depletion, water consumption, land use changes, and other environmental indicators. They follow standardized methodologies like ISO 14040/44 and are regularly updated to reflect technological advances and improved data quality. Regional databases like the European Life Cycle Database (ELCD) or the U.S. Life Cycle Inventory Database (USLCI) provide location-specific environmental impact factors. These databases are essential for conducting scientifically sound LCA calculations during product configuration and enable the comparison of different material choices based on their environmental impacts.

**AAS-Based Data Provider**

The Asset Administration Shell (AAS)[6] is a standardized digital representation of a physical or logical asset, as promoted by the Industrial Digital Twin Association (IDTA) in Germany [11]. The AAS encapsulates all relevant data and services across the asset's lifecycle, providing a digital twin of a product. AAS supports a modular structure through sub-models, which can represent specific sustainability aspects such as carbon footprint or recyclability scores of a component. Thus, AAS-based services can be used to expose sustainability data as part of a product configuration.

---

[4] https://sphera.com/.

[5] https://ecoinvent.org/database/.

[6] https://reference.opcfoundation.org/I4AAS/v100/docs/4.1.

**Digital Product Passports from 3rd Parties**

The Digital Product Passport (DPP) is a standardized, uniquely identifiable, digital record of a product introduced by the UN (as part of the UN Transparency Protocol [22]) and currently adopted by the European Union as part of its ecodesign regulations [18]. It shall facilitate the sharing of product information among the stakeholders of a product's lifecycle by providing—among other things—highly granular, structured, machine-readable data on circularity-related product parameters such as material composition, substances of concern, environmental impacts, repairability, and end of life (EoL) treatment. Leveraging DPP data within the configuration process enables more informed, sustainable product choices, especially when selecting materials and components from 3rd party providers during the manufacturing phase.

**LCA Service**

A Life Cycle Assessment (LCA) service evaluates the environmental impact of products across their entire lifecycle—from raw material extraction to end-of-life. In product configuration, it enables the calculation of product-specific environmental impact indicators such as carbon footprint, energy use, and water consumption for different variants along pre-specified product category rules [12]. This allows for instant feedback on the sustainability impact of user decisions and supports environmentally responsible choices. LCA services also provide verified data for integration into Digital Product Passports (DPPs), ensure compliance with regulations like the ESPR, and can generate standardized documentation such as ISO 14025 compliant Environmental Product Declarations (EPDs) or Product Environmental Footprints (PEFs) as mandated by the European Union [8]. Overall, they support informed decision-making for eco-design and sustainability optimization.

## 9.2 A Sustainability-Enhanced Configuration Model

The evolution of product configuration systems reflects a significant shift in focus over time. While early configurators primarily concentrated on ensuring technical feasibility—configurators were designed to validate whether a specific combination of components could function together effectively from a technical perspective—modern configuration approaches have expanded to address multiple optimization criteria. Today's configuration systems take a more comprehensive approach, considering various optimization goals beyond technical requirements. These include economic factors such as cost minimization, operational aspects like energy efficiency, and practical considerations such as ease of maintenance and serviceability. The optimization criteria have further evolved to include environmental impact, resource efficiency, and lifecycle considerations.

By incorporating sustainability metrics into the configuration process, organizations can optimize their products for both performance and environmental responsibility. This includes considerations such as carbon footprint, material recyclability, energy efficiency during operation, and the overall environmental impact throughout the product's lifecycle. The goal is to find configurations that balance technical requirements, economic viability, and environmental sustainability in an integrated way.

In the following, we will make the information needed for sustainable product configuration more explicit. This way we can provide feedback on how user decisions influence the sustainability of the configured product. We cannot expect to assess the sustainability of a configured product in the same detail as it is done in a full lifecycle assessment process (LCA). Still, our main goals are:

- Compare configurations based on environmental KPIs across lifecycle phases
- Verify compliance with environmental regulations
- Allow specification of material constraints (e.g., hazardous substance restrictions)
- Identify key components and phases with the highest sustainability impact
- Evaluate the impact of various usage scenarios
- Represent end-of-life, recycling, and circular economy options.

**Example SITOP PSU8600 Power Supply System**

As a running example, we use the task of configuring the industrial SITOP PSU8600 power supply system by Siemens.[7]

A SITOP PSU8600 variant comprises multiple components called modules that can be combined according to defined technical constraints. The UML class diagram in Fig. 9.1 illustrates the components of the SITOP PSU8600 system considered in this chapter and their interrelationships. Each SITOP PSU8600 system requires exactly one basic module. Up to four expansion modules can be added to the system. To safeguard the system against small power failures (up to several seconds) buffer modules can be added. For longer power outages, Uninterruptible Power Supply (UPS) modules with a maximum of five batteries are possible. However, the sum of buffer and UPS modules can be at most two.

**Materials**

The material composition is an important part of the sustainability of a product. In the manufacturing phase, the used materials impact the KPIs, e.g., $CO_2$ emissions caused by providing the material. Problematic and hazardous substances impact the end-of-life phase. The materials of a component might either be fixed for supplied parts or variable for generic components, e.g., components whose dimensions can be configured. Figure 9.2 depicts a configuration model augmented with material information. To keep the model simple, the class Component represents anything from products or assemblies to supplied (hardware) parts. Components can have materials and sub-components.

---

[7] See the SITOP PSU8600 product information at: https://mall.industry.siemens.com/mall/en/WW/Catalog/Products/10251281.

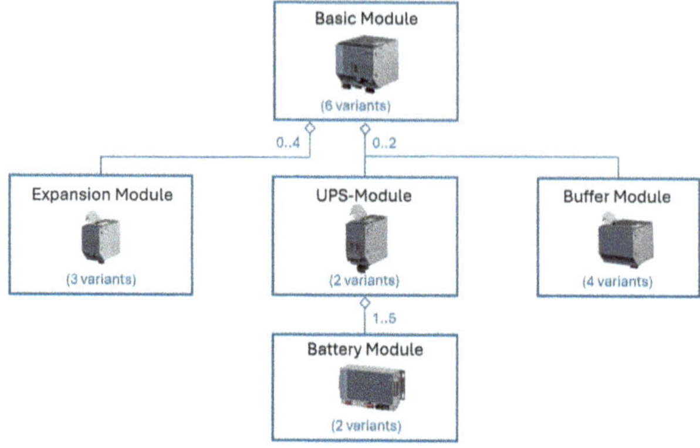


**Fig. 9.1** SITOP PSU8600 UML diagram (*Source* [20])

**Fig. 9.2** Configuration model with materials (*Source* [20])

LCAScope defines the lifecycle phases (LCAPhase) considered in the current Configuration. The class Material defines the amount of a material used in a component.

Each component is composed of an arbitrary number of materials. The level of granularity regarding the used materials depends on the available information. In cases where the material composition of sub-components is not known, the material information of a component just contains the aggregated values of the used materials in the sub-components. The aggregated materials of the whole configuration correspond to the material composition that is reported in EPDs. For instance, in the PLM model (Siemens Teamcenter) the SITOP PSU8600 basic module of a given type is comprised of hundreds of sub-components, such as electronic parts, housing, and so forth.

This detailed information is only relevant if there are some constraints on the sub-components or the user wants to have insights into the material composition of the product. An simplified example for the material composition (BOM) of a SITOP PSU8600 basic module is shown in Fig. 9.3. The information about the materials is taken from the EPD of the basic module and lists the different types of materials and their weights.

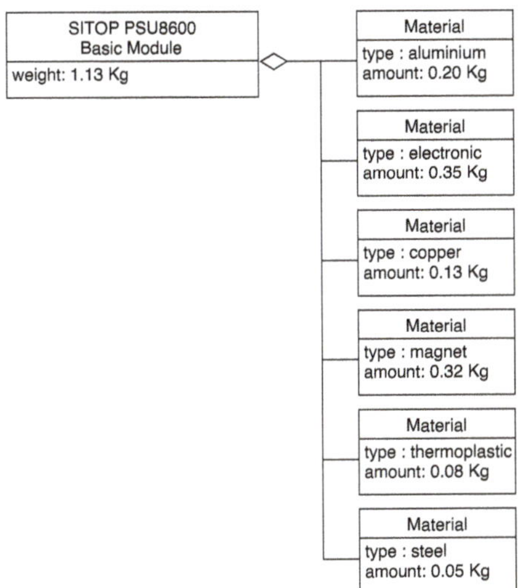


**Fig. 9.3** Basic module material example (*Source* [20])

## Life cycle stages and reference scenarios

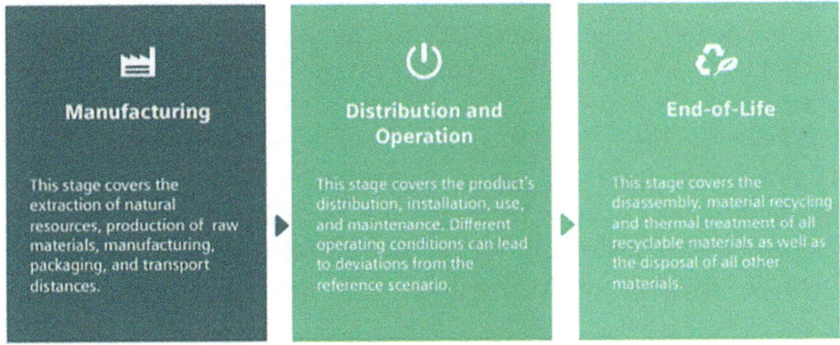


**Fig. 9.4** SITOP PSU8600 lifecycle phases (as defined in the EPD) (*Source* [20])

### KPIs and Lifecycle Phases

Another important aspect of LCAs and EPDs are key (environmental) performance indicators (KPI). They indicate the environmental impact and resource consumption of the configured product during specific lifecycle phases.

For the running example of this chapter, we use the lifecycle model of the EPDs of the SITOP PSU8600 system[8] (Fig. 9.4). In the EPD, different phases are aggregated into one stage. For example, raw material extraction, production of raw materials, manufacturing, packaging, and transport are summarized in one manufacturing stage.

---

[8] The EPD can be downloaded from https://support.industry.siemens.com/cs/ww/en/view/109824794.

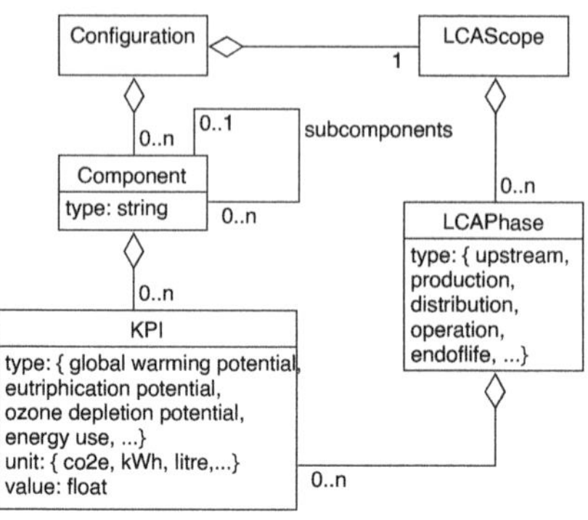



**Fig. 9.5** Configuration model with KPIs (*Source* [20])

The LCA of a product typically covers the entire lifecycle. In a product configurator, not every lifecycle phase will be considered depending on the configuration scenario.

For instance, in a sales configurator, the manufacturing phase and the usage phase are the most important phases. Information about the detailed end-of-life options is very customer-specific and may not be available to the sales configurator. However, at least information about the circularity and recyclability of the product can be provided. In contrast, in an in-house engineering configurator, not only the usage but also circularity and end-of-life aspects are typically known as they are managed inside the organization.

As can be seen in Fig. 9.5, a KPI is assigned to a component and a LCA phase. On the configuration level, these values are aggregated to KPIs per lifecycle phase and subsequently a total KPI can be computed. For our SITOP example, the estimation of the global warming potential (GWP) of the manufacturing phase of the configured SITOP PSU8600 system is the sum of the (manufacturing) GWPs of the components used in the configuration.

## Manufacturing

For supplied components/products, we can expect to get data from existing EPDs or, if available, from a DPP (on the model level). In the case of the SITOP PSU8600 system, the data can be taken from the published EPDs or from in-house tools like the green digital twin (GDT) [25].

In the case of third-party components where this data is not available, we could still use approximate data for the type of product from environmental databases. The data is expected to be more accurate if a more specific type of product is considered. For the estimation of KPIs related to transportation, information is required about the shipping routes for the supplied parts and materials as well as the location where the configured product is assembled. Data for common ways of transportation (air, container ship, rail) are standard in all environmental databases and LCA tools.

The KPIs for production of raw materials and manufacturing the configured product can range from simple (consumer products) to highly complex, e.g., the production of a configured railway interlocking system. The LCA of complex systems involves additional factors like construction work, road work, and specialized equipment. Modeling this information within a product configuration scenario is unrealistic. Therefore, a product configurator must either access data from existing (parametrized) LCA calculations or rely on rough estimates.

**Distribution and Operation**

The transportation aspect of distribution is essentially the same as previously discussed in the manufacturing phases. An additional aspect is packaging, which requires additional (hopefully recyclable or reusable) material.

The impact of the usage phase is very specific to the configured product and the intended usage of the configured system. This is the phase where user requirements typically have the greatest impact. The KPIs for the usage phase are often specified for a defined time period (e.g., 10 years) and usage scenario (e.g., 24/7 operation). For electrical components, the most basic calculation of the GWP is the energy demand of the component multiplied by the usage time multiplied by the GWP of the energy source. However, the situation is more complex in practice. Under a naive calculation, a configuration with fewer components will have a better GWP KPI. But introducing components such as buffer modules increases the reliability of the entire system. Without buffer modules, short drops in electricity (brownouts) can lead to failures in industrial processes and negatively impact the sustainability of the production process as a whole. One way to communicate this to the user is through multi-objective optimization; specifically, showing the relationship between system reliability and sustainability in the case mentioned above.

For long-running systems, obsolescence considerations are a critical aspect of this phase, particularly in determining the number of components that will require replacement within the given time frame based on their expected life expectancy. Repairability and spare parts availability significantly influence the usage phase. However, developing metrics to quantify these aspects remains challenging. Upcoming standards like the DPP will define some standard KPIs to measure these circularity aspects.

**End of Life**

A more sustainable option than simple disposal is to disassemble the product and recycle as much as possible [10, 23, 24]. And even better is one of the R-strategies of the circular economy [16], i.e., reuse, remanufacture, or refurbish should be applied to the product or its sub-components.

## Example

In this section, we show an exemplary implementation of the SITOP example in MiniZinc. The encoding is simple and only serves the purpose of illustrating the sustainability-enhanced aspects of the configuration model. There are many different ways to encode the same problem in MiniZinc; see Chap. 5 for more examples. In other modeling paradigms or in commercial tools, the models will look different. The used ideas, however, are valid independently of the concretely used modeling approach.

The purpose of the encodings below is to sketch a concrete implementation of these general ideas to incorporate sustainability aspects in product configuration. In practice, user decisions (parameters) should be clearly distinguished from solver decisions (decision variables), appropriate optimization statements should be defined, and so on. The concrete design choices in these regards are very application-specific and out of scope of this chapter.

### Components and BOM Generation

Listing 9.1 shows how components and their quantities are encoded for the SITOP PSU8600 example. The cardinality constraints are taken from Fig. 9.1.

```
1  enum SITOPComponent = {
2    BaseModule,
3    ExpansionModule,
4    BufferModule,
5    UPSModule,
6    BatteryModule };
7
8  array[SITOPComponent] of var 0..10:
       component_quantity;
9
10 var 0..5: UPSModule1_nrofbatteries;
11 var 0..5: UPSModule2_nrofbatteries;
12
13 constraint component_quantity[BaseModule] = 1;
14 constraint component_quantity[ExpansionModule]
       <= 4;
15
16 constraint component_quantity[BufferModule] +
       component_quantity[UPSModule] <= 2;
17
18 constraint UPSModule1_nrofbatteries >0 <->
       component_quantity[UPSModule] = 1;
19
20 constraint UPSModule2_nrofbatteries >0 <->
       component_quantity[UPSModule] = 2;
21
22 constraint component_quantity[BatteryModule] =
       UPSModule1_nrofbatteries +
       UPSModule2_nrofbatteries;
```

**Listing 9.1** MiniZinc encoding of components

## Encoding of Materials

 The materials of components are modeled with a table that contains the amount of material included in every component. This amount is considered fixed, i.e., for this simple example, there is no variability. In a more realistic example, the dimension of a component might be configurable, e.g., the length of a cable, and therefore the materials would also be dynamic. Based on the selected components and the material table, the total amount is computed. This allows the easy formulation of constraints about the material content of the configuration, like the one in Listing 9.2 which states that the configuration should not contain any hazardous materials.

```
 1  enum Material = {
 2    aluminium,
 3    electronic,
 4    copper,
 5    steel,
 6    lead };
 7
 8  % example configuration - one basic module
 9  component_quantity = [1,0,0,0,0];
10
11  array[int] of record
12    (SITOPComponent:component, Material: material,
          int: gram):
13    material_table = [
14    (component: BaseModule, material: aluminium,
          gram:20),
15    (component: BaseModule, material: electronic,
          gram:35),
16    (component: BaseModule, material: copper,
          gram:13),
17    %...
18  ];
19
20  array[Material] of var int:
         total_weight_material;
21
22  constraint forall (m in Material)
23    (total_weight_material[m] = sum([
24      row.gram * component_quantity[row.component]
            |
25      row in material_table where row.material = m
26    ]));
27
28  var set of Material: hazardous_materials = {
         lead };
29
30  % example: configuration should contain no
         hazardous materials
31  constraint forall (m in Material)
32    (total_weight_material[m]>0 ->
33      not (m in hazardous_materials)
34    );
```

**Listing 9.2** MiniZinc encoding of materials

**Distribution**

For the distribution phase, we can model the impact of transporting the final product
from the assembly location to the customer. This involves defining different modes
of transport, their respective environmental impact factors (e.g., kg $CO_2$-eq per ton-
kilometer), and the total weight of the configured system. Listing 9.3 shows a simple
implementation where the model can choose a transport mode based on user requirements or optimization goals.

```minizinc
% available transport modes
enum TransportMode = {TRUCK, TRAIN, AIR};

% transport mode
var TransportMode: transport_mode;

% GWP in kg CO2-eq per ton-km for each transport
    mode
array[TransportMode] of float:
  transport_gwp_factor = [0.08, 0.02, 0.5];

% distance to customer in km (can be a user
    requirement)
float: distance_km = 1000.0;

% total weight in kg (calculated from materials)
var float: total_weight_gram =
  sum(m in Material) (total_weight_material[m]);

% calculated GWP for the distribution phase
var float: distribution_gwp =
  transport_gwp_factor[transport_mode] *
      (total_weight_gram / 1000.0) * distance_km;

% example constraint: urgent deliveries require
    air freight
% constraint transport_mode = AIR;
```

**Listing 9.3** MiniZinc encoding of distribution

**Usage**

The impact of the usage phase is highly dependent on the efficiency of the product
and the operating scenario of the user. For the SITOP PSU8600, the primary environmental impact during usage stems from energy loss (heat dissipation), not the
energy it delivers to other components. We can calculate this by taking the energy
consumed by the power supply itself and multiplying it by an impact factor for the
electricity grid. Listing 9.4 demonstrates this calculation.

```
1  % efficiency of the basic module (can depend on
       selected type)
2  par float: base_module_efficiency = 0.95;
3
4  % user requirements for usage profile
5  par float: avg_power_output_kw = 2.0; % Avg.
       power delivered
6  par float: lifetime_h = 43800; % e.g., 5 years
       of 24/7 ops
7
8  % environmental factor for the electricity grid
       (e.g., from EPD or database), kg CO2-eq per
       kWh
9  par float: grid_gwp_factor = 0.4;
10
11 % total energy delivered over the lifetime
12 var float: total_energy_delivered_kwh =
13   avg_power_output_kw * lifetime_h;
14
15 % total energy consumed by the PSU
16 var float: total_energy_consumed_kwh =
17   total_energy_delivered_kwh /
         base_module_efficiency;
18
19 % total energy lost as heat
20 var float: energy_loss_kwh =
21   total_energy_consumed_kwh -
         total_energy_delivered_kwh;
22
23 % calculated GWP for the usage phase
24 var float: usage_gwp = energy_loss_kwh *
       grid_gwp_factor;
```

**Listing 9.4** MiniZinc encoding of usage

## End of Life

The end-of-life phase considers the environmental effects of disposing of, recycling, or reusing the product's materials. Different treatments yield different impacts; for instance, recycling metal often results in an environmental credit, avoiding emissions from raw material production. Listing 9.5 models this by allowing a choice of end-of-life option for each material and calculating the resulting environmental impact. The effects of more sophisticated R-strategies like reuse, remanufacturing, refurbish on the GWP are too difficult to calculate in a configuration model. Regardless, components to which these R-strategies can be applied should be preferred in the configuration either by modeling the options as boolean or giving them an "estimated" GWP value that is lower than the other EoL options.

```
1  % End-of-Life options
2  enum EoL_Option = {LANDFILL, INCINERATION,
       RECYCLING};
3
4  % choose an EoL option for each material
5  array[Material] of var EoL_Option: eol_choice;
6
7  % GWP impact per kg of material for each EoL
       option (kg CO2-eq/kg).
8  % negative values represent credits from
       recycling.
9  % this data would come from LCA databases.
10 array[Material, EoL_Option] of float:
       eol_gwp_matrix =
11   [| % Columns: LANDFILL, INCINERATION, RECYCLING
12     0.02, 0.05, -1.5,   % for Aluminium
13   | 0.05, 0.20, -0.8,   % for Electronics
       (simplified)
14   | 0.02, 0.04, -2.8,   % for Copper
15   | 0.04, 0.06, -3.5,   % for Steel
16   | 0.5, 0.70, 0.70,    % for Lead
17   %...
18   |];
19
20 % calculated GWP for the end-of-life phase
21 var float: eol_gwp = sum(m in Material)
       ((total_weight_material[m] / 1000.0) *
       eol_gwp_matrix[m, eol_choice[m]]);
22
23 % example constraint: Maximize recycling
24 constraint forall(m in {aluminium, copper,
       steel}) (eol_choice[m] = RECYCLING);
```

**Listing 9.5** MiniZinc encoding of end-of-life

**Solving**

The encodings in Listings 9.1, 9.2, 9.3, 9.4 and 9.5 contain exemplary input parameters, decision variables, and constraints. When solved together, one possible solver output looks as follows:

```
1  component_quantity = [1, 0, 0, 0, 0];
2  transport_mode = TRUCK;
3  total_weight_gram = 68.0;
4  distribution_gwp = 5.44;
5  usage_gwp = 1844.210526315792;
6  eol_gwp = -0.0646499999999999;
```

This is an assignment of concrete values to decision variables and can be interpreted as one valid configuration.[9]

---

[9] Output has been customized to show selected variable assignments using output statements.

## Exercises

**Exercise 9.1** Greenhouse gas emissions are associated with one of three scopes in greenhouse gas reporting [28]. Conduct some research to find out which product-related activities are associated with which scope and identify those activities where product configuration can influence emissions, and how product configuration can help reduce emissions.

**Exercise 9.2** Consider the example use case of configuring an elevator.[10] We are a CPQ solution provider, implementing constraint-based configurators for our customers (B2B). Our customer is an international corporation producing and selling elevators to its customers (end customers).

To evaluate our offering, our customer wants to see a prototype with the following characteristics:

- two main components of interest for the prototype: car and motor
- different materials may be used for the car (e.g., steel/recycled aluminium)
- if the total weight (including passengers) is high, a strong motor must be used, otherwise a weak motor can be used
- the electricity consumption in the usage phase depends on the usage intensity and on the type of motor
- the environmental footprint in the usage phase depends on the electricity consumption and on the energy mix of the electricity supplier
- the installation site will be known (e.g., a hotel in Vienna)
- the elevator can be produced in a factory in Vienna or in Shanghai
- the elevator can be delivered to the end-customer by different means (truck, ship, cargo plane).

Describe the characteristics of the configuration problem (decision variables, other variables, pseudo-code constraints, optimization criteria, …). List all end-customer decisions that influence the sustainability of the product.

**Exercise 9.3** Based on Sect. 9.2, develop a few user stories[11] for a configurator for elevators where the user is a business purchaser. How will the user want to use the configurator to configure a product that meets various requirements?

**Exercise 9.4** Come up with your own ideas for what features the configurator (GUI) should exhibit to optimally support the user in configuring an environmentally friendly and cost-efficient product (make sure to consider the user stories from Sect. 9.3).

**Exercise 9.5** Develop a MiniZinc or ASP encoding (cf. Chap. 5) for the elevator use case from Sect. 9.2, similar to the MiniZinc example in this chapter.

---

[10] This example is heavily inspired by a use case from Tacton [21].

[11] In software development, a user story is an informal description of a feature from the perspective of a user.

**Exercise 9.6** Consider the folding bike example used throughout this book, and in particular the electric folding bike from Chap. 3 that includes a motor and a battery. Sketch how all LCA aspects discussed in this chapter could be reflected in this example. Extend the sales view and parts view from Chap. 3 appropriately.

# References


1. Campo Gay, I., Hvam, L.: Sustainability-focused product configurators benefits and expectations: a construction industry case. In: IEEE International Conference on Industrial Engineering and Engineering Management. IEEE (2023). https://doi.org/10.1109/ieem58616.2023.10406559
2. Campo Gay, I., Hvam, L., Haug, A.: Automation of life cycle assessment through configurators. In: Z. Anišić, C. Forza (eds.) 10th International Conference on Mass Customization and Personalization, pp. 19–25 (2022). https://mcp-ce.org/wp-content/uploads/2022/10/5.pdf
3. Communication from the commission to the European Parliament, the Council, the European Economic and Social Committee and the Committee of the Regions. The European Green Deal (2019). https://eur-lex.europa.eu/legal-content/EN/TXT/?uri=CELEX:52019DC0640
4. Communication from the commission to the European Parliament, the Council, the European Economic and Social Committee and the Committee of the Regions. A New Circular Economy Action Plan for a Cleaner and More Competitive Europe. Technical Report. COM/2020/98 final, European Union (2020). https://eur-lex.europa.eu/legal-content/EN/TXT/?uri=CELEX:52020DC0098
5. Communication from the commission to the European Parliament, the Council, the European Economic and Social Committee and the Committee of the Regions. A Green Deal Industrial Plan for the Net-Zero Age. Technical Report. COM/2023/62 final, European Union (2023). https://eur-lex.europa.eu/legal-content/EN/TXT/?uri=CELEX:52023DC0062
6. Communication from the commission to the European Parliament, the Council, the European Economic and Social Committee and the Committee of the Regions. The clean industrial deal: a joint roadmap for competitiveness and decarbonisation (2025). https://eur-lex.europa.eu/legal-content/EN/TXT/?uri=CELEX:52025DC0085
7. Conference of the Parties: Adoption of the Paris Agreement (2015). https://unfccc.int/resource/docs/2015/cop21/eng/l09r01.pdf
8. European Commission: PEF METHOD - European Commission (2025). https://green-forum.ec.europa.eu/environmental-footprint-methods/pef-method_en
9. Falkner, A.A., Comploi-Taupe, R., Müller, K., Rogenhofer, S.: Requirements and architectures for green configuration. In: Vareilles, É., Grosso, C., Horcas, J.M., Felfernig, A. (eds.) Proceedings of the 26th International Workshop on Configuration (ConfWS 2024) co-located with the 30th International Conference on Principles and Practice of Constraint Programming (CP 2024), Girona, Spain, September 2–3, 2024, CEUR Workshop Proceedings, vol. 3812, pp. 33–40. CEUR-WS.org (2024). https://ceur-ws.org/Vol-3812/paper5.pdf
10. Gungor, A., Gupta, S.M.: Issues in environmentally conscious manufacturing and product recovery: a survey. Comput. Ind. Eng. **36**(4), 811–853 (1999). https://doi.org/10.1016/S0360-8352(99)00167-9
11. Industrial Digital Twin Association: Asset Administration Shell (2025). https://industrialdigitaltwin.org/
12. International EPD System: The PCR | EPD International (2025). https://www.environdec.com/pcr/the-pcr
13. ISO: ISO 14040:2006 - Environmental management - Life cycle assessment - Principles and framework (2025). https://www.iso.org/standard/37456.html
14. ISO: ISO 14044:2006 - Environmental management - Life cycle assessment - Requirements and guidelines (2025). https://www.iso.org/standard/38498.html

15. Jakobsen, A., Tambo, T., Kadenic, M.: Greener information systems for product configuration management: towards adaptation to sustainability requirements. In: Proceedings of the 26th International Conference on Enterprise Information Systems, pp. 100–109. SCITEPRESS - Science and Technology Publications, Angers, France (2024). https://doi.org/10.5220/0012737200003690

16. Morseletto, P.: Targets for a circular economy. Resour. Conserv. Recycl. **153**, 104553 (2020). https://doi.org/10.1016/j.resconrec.2019.104553

17. Nethercote, N., Stuckey, P.J., Becket, R., Brand, S., Duck, G.J., Tack, G.: MiniZinc: towards a standard CP modelling language. In: Bessiere, C. (ed.) Principles and Practice of Constraint Programming - CP 2007, 13th International Conference, CP 2007, Providence, RI, USA, September 23–27, 2007, Proceedings, Lecture Notes in Computer Science, vol. 4741, pp. 529–543. Springer, Berlin (2007). https://doi.org/10.1007/978-3-540-74970-7_38

18. Regulation (EU) 2024/1781 of the European Parliament and of the Council of 13 June 2024 establishing a framework for the setting of ecodesign requirements for sustainable products, amending Directive (EU) 2020/1828 and Regulation (EU) 2023/1542 and repealing Directive 2009/125/EC (Text with EEA relevance) (2024). http://data.europa.eu/eli/reg/2024/1781/oj

19. Ritchie, H.: Sector by sector: where do global greenhouse gas emissions come from? Our World in Data (2020). https://ourworldindata.org/ghg-emissions-by-sector

20. Schenner, G., Havur, G., Rogenhofer, S., Wallner, S., Filtz, E., Pellegrini, T.: A lifecycle- and sustainability-aware product configuration model for modular industrial systems. In: Vareilles, É., Grosso, C., Sandrin, E., Le, V.M. (eds.) Proceedings of the 27th International Workshop on Configuration (ConfWS 2025) co-located with the 28th European Conference on Artificial Intelligence (ECAI 2025), Bologna, Italy, October 25–26, 2025, CEUR Workshop Proceedings. CEUR-WS.org (2025)

21. Tacton Systems AB: Tacton CPQ environmental footprint configuration (2025). https://www.tacton.com/products/tacton-cpq/environmental-footprint-configuration/

22. United Nations Economic Commission for Europe: UN Transparency Protocol (2025). https://uncefact.github.io/spec-untp/

23. Viswanathan, S., Allada, V.: Configuration analysis to support product redesign for end-of-life disassembly. Int. J. Prod. Res. **39**(8), 1733–1753 (2001). https://doi.org/10.1080/00207540110034887

24. Viswanathan, S., Allada, V.: Product configuration optimization for disassembly planning: a differential approach. Omega **34**(6), 599–616 (2006). https://doi.org/10.1016/j.omega.2005.01.011. Reverse production systems

25. Walczyk, P.: Siemens' green digital twin: a LCA software tool used by over 1.200 Siemens users soon available for external users (2025). https://blog.siemens.com/2025/05/siemens-green-digital-twin-a-lca-software-tool-used-by-over-1-200-siemens-users-soon-available-for-external-users/

26. Wiezorek, R., Christensen, N.: Integrating sustainability information in configurators. In: Aldanondo, M., Falkner, A.A., Felfernig, A., Stettinger, M. (eds.) Proceedings of the 23rd International Configuration Workshop (CWS/ConfWS 2021), Vienna, Austria, 16–17 September, 2021, CEUR Workshop Proceedings, vol. 2945, pp. 65–72. CEUR-WS.org (2021). https://ceur-ws.org/Vol-2945/52-RW-ConfWS21_paper_16.pdf

27. Wikipedia contributors: Sustainability – Wikipedia, the free encyclopedia. https://en.wikipedia.org/w/index.php?title=Sustainability&oldid=1312615889 (2025)

28. World Resources Institute and World Business Council for Sustainable Development: The greenhouse gas protocol: a corporate accounting and reporting standard (2024). https://ghgprotocol.org/corporate-standard

**Open Access** This chapter is licensed under the terms of the Creative Commons Attribution-NonCommercial-NoDerivatives 4.0 International License (http://creativecommons.org/licenses/by-nc-nd/4.0/), which permits any noncommercial use, sharing, distribution and reproduction in any medium or format, as long as you give appropriate credit to the original author(s) and the source, provide a link to the Creative Commons license and indicate if you modified the licensed material. You do not have permission under this license to share adapted material derived from this chapter or parts of it.

The images or other third party material in this chapter are included in the chapter's Creative Commons license, unless indicated otherwise in a credit line to the material. If material is not included in the chapter's Creative Commons license and your intended use is not permitted by statutory regulation or exceeds the permitted use, you will need to obtain permission directly from the copyright holder.

GPSR Compliance
The European Union's (EU) General Product Safety Regulation (GPSR) is a set
of rules that requires consumer products to be safe and our obligations to
ensure this.

If you have any concerns about our products, you can contact us on

ProductSafety@springernature.com

In case Publisher is established outside the EU, the EU authorized
representative is:

Springer Nature Customer Service Center GmbH
Europaplatz 3
69115 Heidelberg, Germany

www.ingramcontent.com/pod-product-compliance
Ingram Content Group UK Ltd.
Pitfield, Milton Keynes, MK11 3LW, UK
UKHW020813080726
473059UK00007B/2209